Love, Loss, and Abjection

Love, Loss, and Abjection

The Journey of New Birth in the Gospel of John

Melanie Baffes

☙PICKWICK Publications • Eugene, Oregon

LOVE, LOSS, AND ABJECTION
The Journey of New Birth in the Gospel of John

Copyright © 2016 Melanie Baffes. All rights reserved. Except for brief quotations in critical publications or reviews, no part of this book may be reproduced in any manner without prior written permission from the publisher. Write: Permissions, Wipf and Stock Publishers, 199 W. 8th Ave., Suite 3, Eugene, OR 97401.

Pickwick Publications
An Imprint of Wipf and Stock Publishers
199 W. 8th Ave., Suite 3
Eugene, OR 97401

www.wipfandstock.com

Paperback ISBN: 978-1-4982-8410-3
Hardcover ISBN: 978-1-4982-8412-7
Ebook ISBN: 978-1-4982-8411-0

Cataloguing-in-Publication data:

Names: Baffes, Melanie.

Title: Love, loss, and abjection : the journey of new birth in the Gospel of John / Melanie Baffes.

Description: Eugene, OR: Pickwick Publications, 2016 | Includes bibligraphical references and index.

Identifiers: ISBN: 978-1-4982-8410-3 (paperback) | ISBN: 978-1-4982-8412-7 (hardback) | ISBN: 978-1-4982-8411-0 (ebook)

Subjects: 1. Bible. John—Criticism, interpretation, etc. 2. Lazarus of Bethany, Saint. 3. Bible. New Testament—Psychology. I. Title.

Classification: BS2615.2 B28 2016 (print) | CALL NUMBER (ebook)

Manufactured in the U.S.A.

Contents

Acknowledgments | vii
Introduction: The Fourth Evangelist's Understanding of Humanity | 1
1 Rebirth through the Lens of Psychoanalytic Theory | 15
2 The World as Illusion—John 11:1–37 | 42
3 The Boundary of Transformation—John 11:38–45 | 82
4 A Radically Different Life—John 12:1–8 | 102
5 The Journey of New Birth | 128

APPENDIX: *Subjectivity in Psychoanalytic Theory and Rebirth in the Gospel of John* | 135

Bibliography | 137
Index | 145

Acknowledgments

I would like to express profound gratitude to several colleagues who guided me in this unconventional exploration of John's gospel. Dr. Seung Ai Yang introduced me to a breadth of hermeneutical approaches for reading the biblical text and went above and beyond to provide moral support in the early days of my research. Dr. Lallene Rector sparked my passion for psychology/psychoanalytic theory and offered invaluable guidance as I slowly found my niche. And Advisor Dr. K. K. Yeo listened patiently while my ideas took shape and skillfully guided me toward a productive project—all the time modeling brilliant scholarship, humility, and kindness. All three offered invaluable insights that have enriched this project in numerous ways.

I also want to thank other scholars who supported me in this endeavor: Dr. Diane Capitani, co-author and friend; Dr. Osvaldo Vena, professor and fellow biblical scholar; and Dr. Angela Cowser, writing partner and coach. These professors were (and are) the best colleagues, mentors, and conversation partners an emerging scholar could ever hope for, and I am grateful for the spirit and authenticity they bring to their scholarship.

Finally, my gratitude goes out to Rev. Julie Johnson, Rev. Rockwell Ward, and Rev. Dr. John Philip Newell, all of whom accompanied me on various legs of my journey to Christianity. Each of them taught me what it means to be made in the image of God, and each helped me see that questioning our beliefs, rather than being an indication of weakness, is actually a sign of deep engagement and, ultimately, genuine faith.

Introduction
The Fourth Evangelist's Understanding of Humanity

In the four decades since Walter Wink first made his now-famous claim that "historical biblical criticism is bankrupt," the field has expanded exponentially to recognize a variety of interpretive approaches, many of which have given voice to individuals and groups ignored by traditional methods. Biblical criticism increasingly has been de-centered, and no single approach shapes our understanding of the text. Yet the essence of Wink's original claim still stands: the science of biblical criticism has objectified the text to such an extent that it creates a "split consciousness" in believers; we study the text as an object to be mastered and, in doing so, we become alienated from its transformative power. But this alienation, Wink claims, "is the twin of another: our own alienation, in the act of scholarship, from ourselves."[1] In any interpretation of the biblical text, we limit ourselves to asking only those questions that can be answered by the methods we have chosen and must therefore set aside the essential questions "on which full human life depends."[2] In fact, it is the understanding of human life, in Wink's view, that is the very substance of the gospel: "Jesus' teaching was not just that we should be free, but that we should be *human*. Oppression, poverty, and suffering inhibit our freedom to move on to the real point of the gospel: to become fully human beings."[3]

For Wink, the solution lies not in rejecting traditional methods of biblical criticism, but in combining them with an approach that takes seriously the ways in which modern readers are conditioned to read the text, an approach that allows them to struggle with the radical, life-challenging questions we have set aside. Only then will we be able to interpret the biblical

---

1. Wink, *Bible in Human Transformation*, 31–32.
2. Ibid., 7, 37.
3. Ibid., vii.

text in such a way that it can enliven the past and "illumine our present with new possibilities for personal and social transformation."[4]

Wink's critique has particular resonance for my interest in the Fourth Gospel and the question that underlies this project: *What can John's gospel tell us about what it means to be fully human?* If Wink is correct in claiming that Jesus' message in the gospels is about being human, John's gospel is a fitting place to look for evidence. One obvious reason is that the author of John depicts a profound separation between the divine and human realms. In his vision of the cosmos, John situates humanity in the world below, an earthly realm in which humans are enslaved to the powers of sin, death, and darkness. These powers operate in opposition to the world above, the heavenly realm of God in which light and life conquer death and darkness. The ultimate purpose of John's "two-worlds" construct is to reveal the power of God over the hostile forces of the world below, and it is through this competing-powers imagery that John clearly establishes a relationship of domination between the divine and human realms.[5]

If humans are understood as standing in opposition to God—alienated from life, light, and truth, and in bondage to darkness, death, sin, slavery, and falsehood—the possibilities for human existence are limited at best. More than forty years ago, Mary Daly asserted that the concept of God as a transcendent Supreme Being who controls the world according to his will keeps humans in a state of subordination and "infantile subjection."[6] In John's gospel, although humans do have access to union with God—a privilege innately theirs from birth by virtue of having been made in God's image—at the same time, there is in humanity a deep dividedness and an inability to connect with God. From this perspective, humans are unaware of their longing for a deeper reality and are not living the fullness of life that is possible for them.

Even more problematic, as feminist scholars have argued for decades, an ideology of domination like the one in John's gospel is a dangerous model. Elisabeth Schüssler Fiorenza points out that promoting a worldview of "power over" shapes our understanding not only of our relationship to God but also our relationship to other humans. If God is king, monarch, Lord, warrior, divine patriarch, and all-powerful Father who presides over everything, has dominion over his "chosen" people, and demands obedience and

---

4. Ibid., 2, 28–39.
5. O'Day and Hylen, *John*, 14–15; Ridderbos, *John*, 129–31, 149.
6. Daly, *Beyond God the Father*, 16–18.

submission from those he rules—and if Jesus is the great hero, the savior of the world, or the Son of God to whom humans must respond with love, worship, and sacrificial service—then all relationships are fair game for similar patterns of domination. History has demonstrated that the ethos of "power over" in the biblical text has been used to justify oppression (control, violence, and dehumanization) and Othering (marginalization, exclusion, and alienation)—and will continue to do so unless we find new ways to understand ourselves in relation to the Divine.[7]

Some scholars attempt to resolve the question of humanity's estrangement from God in terms of relationship. In this view, humans are both alienated from God but also have a fundamental need to be connected; the role Jesus plays in atonement (at-one-ment) is to bring humanity back into wholeness and true relationship with God.[8] Feminist scholars, especially, have explored John's gospel in terms of themes such as friendship and love. Sandra Schneiders sees in John an invitation to share in divine love; she understands discipleship and service as acts of self-giving, with the highest form of serving involving not domination or superiority, but instead representing true friendship based on equality.[9] Similarly, Dorothy Lee interprets John's gospel through the lenses of love, friendship, and abiding. She understands the incarnation itself as an outpouring of the primordial love underlying all of creation, a love that overflows into the world and invites humanity into divine friendship. In Lee's view, this love imbues all the relationships in John's gospel with "shared knowledge, trust, and openness in relationship to Jesus, who acts as the true friend."[10] Mary Coloe sees relational themes in the Gospel of John expressed most clearly in the metaphors of family and household. Not only are relationships described in familial terms—Jesus is the Son, "who is close to the Father's heart" and makes God known (1:18), and all who receive and believe in him have "the power to become children of God" (1:12)—but also the language evokes ideas of intimacy, friendship, and family.[11] Closely related to this theme is the idea of dwelling: "In my Father's house there are many dwelling-places"

---

7. Schüssler Fiorenza, *Jesus—Miriam's Child, Sophia's Prophet*, 47; Schüssler Fiorenza, *Power of the Word*, 4–7, 31, 195–200; Daly, *Beyond God the Father*, 31.

8. Koester, "What Does It Mean to Be Human?," 406.

9. Schneiders, "The Foot Washing," 83–87; Schneiders, *Written That You May Believe*, 192–95.

10. Lee, "Friendship, Love, and Abiding," 61.

11. Coloe, *Dwelling in the Household of God*, 131–32; Coloe, "Welcome into the Household," 404–6, 410–14.

4   LOVE, LOSS, AND ABJECTION

(14:2). When Jesus invites the disciples to "Abide in me, as I abide in you" (15:4), the verb μένειν expresses more than just physical dwelling—it also conveys an intimate connection with Jesus, one grounded in the love relationship he shares with the Father.[12]

Postcolonial scholars such as Kwok Pui-lan, Tan Yak-hwee, and Musa Dube explore the divine-human relationship from the perspective of colonialism, paying special attention to the ways in which the imperial ideology has been used historically (and continues to be used) as a tool of oppression. For postcolonial scholars, the "power-over" ethos embedded in John's gospel reflects the experience of imperialism, and they seek to deconstruct this ideology by revealing the dynamics of inclusion and exclusion, center and margin, Self and Other. By exploring themes such as immigration, exile, migrancy, diaspora, displaced cultures, and border-crossing, postcolonial scholars call attention to the Western bias of traditional interpretations, revealing the idea of one truth above all others as a hierarchical construct of patriarchy. Each of these scholars encourages readers to understand the biblical narrative through their own myths, stories, and experiences and to blend together different cultural traditions in order to conceptualize truths about themselves, their world, and God.[13]

While these interpreters have provided new lenses for understanding the human-divine relationship, their vision of the human person is circumscribed; none of these models acknowledges the importance of selfhood as a foundation for any authentic relationship. In the traditional domination-submission understanding of John's gospel, the human self is subjugated to the primacy of Jesus and God. Yet even in relation-based understandings of John, human personhood is subsumed in community *or* merged in unity with the Divine. And postcolonial models, in attempting to dismantle the hierarchical/imperialist model of relationships, understand the individual in terms of a larger social and political cultural identity. What is missing from these interpretations is an important dimension of human experience: the role of individual selfhood, agency, authority, and responsibility in relationship to community, the world, and to God.

A focus on the individual may seem counter to common understandings of John's gospel, which is generally considered to be one of the church's primary documents on Christian unity. Yet, as Raymond F. Collins argues,

---

12. Coloe, *Dwelling in the Household of God*, 146, 162.

13. Kwok Pui-lan, *Introducing Asian Feminist Theology*, 33–37; Kwok Pui-lan, "Claiming a Boundary Existence," 123–24.

the "depth of the gospel lies in its penetrating analysis of the meaning of the individual's relationship with God in Christ."[14] Similarly, C.F.D. Moule believes the Fourth Gospel to be more profoundly individualistic than any other New Testament writing. As evidence, he points to the fact that there are only four mentions of "the Twelve" (δώδεκα; 6:67; 70; 71; 20:24) in the gospel. In addition, numerous verses speak of the relationship between the Johannine Jesus and individual believers, as in "whoever believes in me will never be thirsty" (6:35). In John, Jesus has numerous encounters with individuals and, in many instances, he interacts differently with various characters, responding to the specific needs and circumstances of that person. Most important, the culmination of all of Jesus' signs in John is the restoration of one individual's life (11:38–44). These clues lead Moule to conclude that John envisions a "one-by-one salvation."[15]

It is clear that, at the same time the evangelist paints a picture of humans as separated from God, he also offers hope for the individual believer. John repeatedly encourages "believing" (alternately expressed as "seeing," "hearing," "listening," "receiving," "following," "abiding," "dwelling," "knowing," and "confessing"), which involves fully accepting God's revelation in Jesus. Humans walk a line between belief and unbelief, what Ruldolf Bultmann calls a "dualism of decision," highlighting the choice they must make between two ways of living[16]—living in the world of darkness and death or choosing the alternative life to which Jesus points, a life in which darkness and death no longer have power over humans. John stresses that only through believing in Jesus can this alternative life be found, and believing in this way is on such a deep level that it can only be thought of as transformative, a new birth.[17] When John says that believers must be "born from above" (γεννηθῇ ἄνωθεν; 3:3, 7), it is a metaphor for being born into this new way of life, not as a one-time choice but as a continuing "transformation to a way of seeing the world in which death no longer captures the human imagination."[18]

While "believing" suggests a choice, an *action*, John's vision of being "born from above" (γεννηθῇ ἄνωθεν; 3:3, 7) expresses a *fundamental change* in the individual, a change that bridges the divide between God

---

14. Collins, *These Things Have Been Written*, 1.
15. Moule, "Individualism of the Fourth Gospel," 171–72, 176, 182–84.
16. Bultmann, *Theology*, 2:21.
17. Smith, *Theology*, 94, 97.
18. O'Day and Hylen, *John*, 15.

6   LOVE, LOSS, AND ABJECTION

and humans. The evangelist describes in detail what it means to be "of this world"—the human being before being born from above—but he provides few clues about what a born-from-above individual looks like and even fewer clues about how this fundamental change comes about.

Mary of Bethany: A Journey of Transformation

The following chapters explore the premise that being born from above can be understood in John's gospel as a journey toward being fully human. Although several characters in the story come to believe in Jesus to varying degrees, I suggest that it is Mary of Bethany who embodies the fundamental change that being born from above signifies. Surprisingly, in reception history, Mary has been overlooked and diminished almost more than any other character in John's gospel. Always living in the shadow of her sister Martha who, because of her complete confession of faith (11:27) is understood as the prototype of female discipleship and leadership among women,[19] Mary often is interpreted as a model of a silent and submissive woman, the one who kneels and weeps in Jesus' presence. Traditional interpreters such as Raymond E. Brown and Rudolf Schnackenburg, for example, see Mary's role as secondary to Martha's participation, suggesting that the scene in which she meets Jesus (11:28–33) is unnecessary because it does not add anything to the story or move the action forward.[20] Similarly, Rudolf Bultmann and Ben Witherington see Mary as exhibiting helplessness and a failure of trust; in their view, Mary has not reached the level of faith and certainty as her sister.[21] Even feminist interpreters such as Sandra M. Schneiders, Adele Reinhartz, and Turid Karlsen Seim privilege Martha as the true disciple, leader, and role model, relegating Mary to being "an echo of Martha" whose sole function is to set the stage for the Jews.[22] Elisabeth Moltmann-Wendel expresses well the reason Mary continues to be overlooked: she "suffers the fate of many women: her voice is not loud, what she says is not original, her story is not dramatic. Her behavior is not noticeable, her conduct is modest."[23]

19. Reinhartz, "From Narrative to History," 177–79.

20. Brown, *John I–XII*, 435; Schnackenburg, *John*, 2:333–34.

21. Bultmann, *John*, 406; Witherington, *Women in the Ministry of Jesus*, 109.

22. Schneiders, "Death in the Community," 53–54; Reinhartz, "From Narrative to History," 175; Seim, "Roles of Women," 71.

23. Moltmann-Wendel, *Women around Jesus*, 53.

But even when Mary is acknowledged as a key player in the anointing story, she is shortchanged; her role is interpreted as a symbol of love, a model for proper discipleship, or a foreshadowing of Jesus' death. Craig R. Koester interprets Mary's anointing in terms of what it symbolizes: an extravagant gesture of love, honor, and devotion toward Jesus in the face of death, a symbol of the gift Jesus is about to give of his own life through crucifixion and death. Koester acknowledges that, on one level, Mary's anointing is associated with serving another but, on a deeper level, he sees it as a symbol of "the kind of love that is to characterize Christian life,"[24] a love and care that transcends ordinary social conventions. Similarly, Amy-Jill Levine claims that Mary's anointing presages the love commandment Jesus gives his disciples in the chapter following (13:34). Several interpreters, including Ernst Haenchen, see Mary's anointing of Jesus as foreshadowing his washing of the disciples' feet (13:5), with an unexpected reversal of serving and being served: Mary serves Jesus and then Jesus serves the disciples. The most generous interpretations see Mary in the role of a prophet, because she alone knows of Jesus' mission and impending fate; she anticipates his death in a prophetic way and anoints him in advance, while his disciples remain unaware of the *kairos* nature of the moment.[25]

Colleen Conway observes that, even when women like Mary in John's gospel are noted for freedom from strict gender roles, being depicted as faithful, and surpassing the male disciples in terms of the values important to the evangelist, what they actually are most noted for is their appropriate response to Jesus and to God. They are "women" to a male God; "they are to be in a subordinate, dependent, but also intimate, relationship with God."[26] It is the women and other marginalized individuals who empty themselves to receive Jesus and God, but nowhere in the text do we see the powerful or the elite doing so—suggesting that those who are submissive in the earthly realm will continue to be submissive in the heavenly realm. Conway's observation accurately characterizes most readings of Mary of Bethany, whose impact is diminished when her role is reduced to serving a function completely separate from who she is as an individual in the story.

These selected interpretations of Mary of Bethany's story also illustrate, as Wink argues, that interpretive methods do govern the questions we ask about a text and the answers we find. If a reading explains what Mary's

---

24. Koester, *Symbolism in the Fourth Gospel*, 127–30, 134.
25. Haenchen, *John 2*, 85; Bultmann, *John*, 416; Michaels, *John*, 669–70.
26. Conway, "Gender Matters in John," 2:102–3.

role means in terms of the plot (Mary as a symbol), in terms of characterization (Mary as a foil or in contrast to the disciples or to Martha), or in terms of the theological message (Mary as a model of loving discipleship or as a foreshadowing of Jesus' fate), how do these interpretations speak to readers today? Modern readers may approach the text with a different set of questions; instead they instead may wonder, as I do: *Why does Mary behave so differently from her sister Martha? Why does Jesus respond the way he does to the two sisters? Why does Mary anoint Jesus' feet and what does it mean to her? And what does it all mean to me?* It is questions like these that we have forgotten to ask, questions whose answers may inform the contemporary reader's self-knowledge and understanding of Jesus.

This study seeks answers to these questions, exploring Mary's transformation by using an emerging method of biblical interpretation: psychological/psychoanalytic criticism.[27] Rather than applying psychoanalytic constructs to Mary's character, I interpret the larger arc of her story from two perspectives. First, I place Mary's story in dialogue with psychoanalytic theories of the development of the human self to reveal similar patterns between the two. Central to this analysis is the work of Julia Kristeva, known for groundbreaking theories in the fields of philosophy, psychoanalytic theory, structural linguistics, and language/literary theory. Most important to this interpretation are several dimensions of Kristeva's psychoanalytic theory: her understanding of how the human self/subject takes shape in infancy, her contention that subjectivity is a work-in-progress, and her insistence on abjection as a catalyst for developing selfhood. Second, I study these patterns within the context of the Johannine idea of new birth to

---

27. Using psychology/psychoanalytic theory as an interpretative lens is not without challenges. Biblical scholar Ilona Rashkow warns of the dangers of analyzing characters for underlying motivations because it is not possible, she argues, to know whether specific personality traits or actions are included to create a character portrait or to further the story line. In addition, because fictional characters, no matter how real they appear, are not actual persons; as a result, there is no clinical data or "living human document." Rashkow, "In Our Image," 105–13. For this reason, psychological biblical criticism has increasingly functioned as a hermeneutical framework that explores both the role of the text in shaping an individual's worldview—and the role of an individual's experience, context, and assumptions in creating meaning from the text. In this complex interplay between the text and reader, the process becomes a hermeneutical "spiral of developing understanding" in which the reader brings pre-interpretations that are continuously reshaped during the reading of the text. Kille, *Psychological Biblical Criticism*, 16–17, 20. This interpretation of Mary of Bethany's story is influenced by psychoanalytic theory and is intended to offer modern readers a fresh perspective on the concept of new birth in John's gospel.

enhance our understanding of what it means to be born from above, the process whereby this happens, and the implications for what it means to be fully human in John's gospel.

As Mary's story unfolds, I hope to reveal that she experiences birth from above, a transformation that results in a new self, a new relationship with her community, and a new relationship with Jesus and God. In this process, it will become clear that Mary moves from being an insider in Jesus' inner circle—whose identity is defined by those around her—to being Other to everyone in her world, to being a newly constituted self whose identity comes from God. It is in Mary's movement from insider to outsider to God-centered self that the transformation is effected.

Chapter 1 reviews contemporary readings of the Johannine concept of new birth and provides a brief introduction to Julia Kristeva's theories of the development of human subjectivity. The two constructs are then placed in dialogue with one another in order to propose an alternative model for understanding birth from above in John. Chapter 2 focuses on John 11:1–37, tracing Mary of Bethany's movement from security to awakening as she experiences the grief related to her brother's death and Jesus' response to this event. In Chapter 3, the emphasis is on John 11:38–45, interpreting Jesus' raising of Lazarus as a ritual of purification, sanctification, and a reversal of Temple sacrifice—but also exploring the impact on Mary of the in-breaking of the Divine she encounters and the new life Jesus offers. Chapter 4 is an investigation of the anointing scene in John 12:1–8, analyzing Mary's transformed selfhood, her renewed relationship with community, and her participation in the life of the Divine. Chapter 5 summarizes Mary's transformation to propose a new definition of the fully human, born-from-above individual.

One of Kristeva's important legacies is her concept of intertextuality, her contention that any meaningful text is "a complex interweaving of voices from a multiplicity of other discourses."[28] For Kristeva, no text is completely self-contained, and its meaning lies not just in the "static structures and products" of the words on the page but in its dependence on other texts and the ways in which these texts relate to one another.[29] At its most basic level, intertextuality involves reading one text in light of another text. By interpreting Mary of Bethany's story intertextually with Kristeva's

---

28. Becker-Leckrone, *Julia Kristeva*, 92, 155–56.
29. Kristeva, *Revolution in Poetic Language*, 60; Kristeva, "Nous Deux," 8.

theories of human subjectivity, this reading suggests new possibilities for understanding new birth and human becoming.

From Text to Reader

Several parallels exist between what characters experience at the story level of John's gospel and what reader-response theory suggests happens in the process of reading the text. On a very basic level, connections between the reading experience and the story level invite readers to form invisible bonds with individuals in the story, identifying with them and their journeys. But, on a deeper level, other parallels exist as well. First, in the act of receiving information from the narrator, readers begin John's gospel with an "insider" status, assuming they know what is happening. Similarly, most characters in the John narrative, upon their initial encounter with Jesus, assume they understand what he is saying and doing.

Yet, as Jeffrey Lloyd Staley argues, the author of John "has built into the narrative a strategy designed to humble those readers who feel that they are on the inside track . . . [that] there is nothing more for them to learn."[30] As readers encounter double-entendres, evocative language, and distortions of time and space, however, they realize there is *other* information they do not have, and they experience ambiguity and confusion, which then forces them into the role of "outsider."[31] Wolfgang Iser points out that ambiguity in a text prompts the reader to engage more fully in the process of reading; readers must fill in the missing pieces themselves and then correct them as they learn more and more on the way to clarity.[32] In John, specifically, readers encounter metaphors, symbols, and irony that at first displace understanding and only later enhance meaning.[33] Here, the reading experience begins to parallel the experiences of many Johannine characters who, through John's distinctive feature of misunderstanding, hear Jesus make an ambiguous or metaphorical statement, respond either on a literal level or miss the meaning entirely, until an explanation is offered by Jesus. This technique is most commonly understood to be "concealed

---

30. Staley, *Print's First Kiss*, 105 n. 48.
31. Ibid.
32. Iser, "Interaction between Text and Reader," 106–19.
33. Kelber, "Metaphysics and Marginality," 139–42.

riddles" John uses to convey a special meaning to insiders that is impenetrable to outsiders.[34]

Readers then begin to move from ambiguity to clarity as their habitual patterns of perception are changed. Literary critics claim that reading a text often prompts readers to make adjustments to their usual patterns of perception and response, moving them to see the discrepancies between their inner, subjective interpretation and an outer, objective reality and encouraging them to "tolerate challenges to the projections arising from the core of one's self."[35] This parallels movement of selected characters in the John text, as they begin to "see" that Jesus refers not to an earthy reality but to a spiritual one, and they begin to grasp the deeper meaning to which he points.

Werner H. Kelber argues that reading as *both* insider and outsider is vital because the idea of difference is built into John's gospel. Jesus as Logos, because he is both "with God" (πρὸς τὸν θεόν; 1:1) and "God" (θεὸς ἦν; 1:1), reflects ambiguity in his identity from the beginning. He is one with God, yet different from God, reflecting an identity manifested in difference. As he takes on an earthly status, then, Jesus becomes even more distinct from God but still retains his nature as "I am from above" (ἐγὼ ἐκ τῶν ἄνω εἰμί; 8:23). His identity in difference finally culminates in his death, an "experience of extreme difference," which is believed to reveal his true glory. Yet, Kelber argues, while these ambiguities challenge readers, motivating their desire to understand John's gospel, at the same time, there is a longing to rise above the mundane to the transcendent, to a knowledge of Jesus' true identity. This double-focused longing is the way the evangelist "invites readers to consider both the literal and figurative meaning," connecting the human realm to the divine realm, and revealing the connection between Self and Other.[36] David Hunter also describes the impact of reading as both insider and outsider:

> When the reader not only reads as insider but also incorporates the outsider's experience of marginalization by struggling to understand, by secretly ruling out painful options or by clinging to an immutable faith, then the reader . . . courageously holds together

---

34. Smith, *Theology*, 113–14.

35. Alcorn and Bracher, "Literature, Psychoanalysis, and the Re-Formation of the Self," 347.

36. Kelber, "Metaphysics and Marginality," 136–42.

ambiguity and meaning, joy and pain, hope and despair in a life of faith.[37]

In addition to the encounter with difference, literary critics claim that in the process of interpreting any text, readers gain a new identity or subjectivity. Norman Holland argues that, in any act of reading, "identity recreates itself," suggesting that it is not a new subjectivity constituted in the process but a replication of one's "identity theme." By this, Holland means that readers find in the elements of a literary work the very situations they most desire or fear and then match those with their own strategies for achieving what they want or overcoming what they fear.[38] Other literary critics, in exploring the psychological impact of literature, argue that in any act of reading, an individual's identity is set aside in order to allow the text to formulate a new subjectivity within.[39] Wolfgang Iser describes the process in this way:

> If reading removes the subject-object division that constitutes all perception, it follows that the reader will be "occupied" by the thoughts of the author, and these in their turn will cause the drawing of new "boundaries." Text and reader no longer confront each other as object and subject, but instead a "division" takes place within the reader himself . . . Every text we read draws a different boundary within our personality, so that the virtual background (the real "me") will take on a different form, according to the theme of the text concerned.[40]

A similar process occurs with characters in John's gospel; the man born blind, for example, relinquishes his former identity as he lets go of his past, releases old ways of thinking, and renounces old habits. He claims a new identity as a disciple of Jesus, forming new boundaries both within himself and in the world around him.

Readers of John's gospel, then, first apprehend the text as an insider, next move to a position of outsider and, finally, gain a new identity and self-understanding as a result of their encounter with the text. This experience in reading the Johannine text calls to mind Paul Ricoeur's dialectic of "*self*

---

37. Hunter, "Marginalising the Majority?," 267–68.

38. Holland, "Unity, Identity, Text, Self," 124–26; Alcorn and Bracher, "Literature, Psychoanalysis, and the Re-Formation of the Self," 342.

39. Alcorn and Bracher, "Literature, Psychoanalysis, and the Re-Formation of the Self," 342.

40. Iser, "Reading Process," 298–99.

and the *other than self* and his contention that Otherness is fundamental to selfhood: "the selfhood of oneself implies otherhood to such an intimate degree that one cannot be thought of without the other, that instead one passes into the other . . ."[41] It is my hope that this proposed interpretation of Mary of Bethany's story—specifically her movement from insider to outsider to God-centered self—may reveal for readers not only the complex interconnectedness of Self and Other but also the possibilities for bridging the human and divine realms. Perhaps by reading Mary of Bethany's journey through this lens, readers will be prompted to experience their own journey from insider to outsider to God-centered self.

---

41. Ricoeur, *Oneself as Another*, 3.

1

Rebirth through the Lens of Psychoanalytic Theory

In the Prologue to John's gospel, readers learn almost immediately that humans "become children of God" (τέκνα θεοῦ γενέσθαι; 1:12) not through ordinary human birth or natural descent, but through a vastly different process of being "born of God" (ἐκ θεοῦ ἐγεννήθησαν; 1:13). The evangelist reveals nothing about how this process occurs, but we are told that it is through receiving the Logos and believing in his name (1:12) that human beings are given the "right" (ἐξουσία) to become God's children.

This idea of a very different kind of birth finds fuller expression in the discourse between Jesus and Nicodemus in the third chapter of John's gospel. In this passage (3:1–21), the Johannine Jesus states plainly that unless a person is "born from above" (γεννηθῇ ἄνωθεν; 3:3, 7)[1] or "born of water and Spirit" (γεννηθῇ ἐξ ὕδατος καὶ πνεύματος; 3:5), it is not possible

---

1. There is no scholarly consensus about the meaning of ἄνωθεν as it appears here; some translate it as "from above," some read it to mean "again," while others propose an ambiguous use that conveys both meanings—in the sense of a "divine begetting that is both new and supernatural." Vellanickal, *Divine Sonship*, 172–73. In general, interpreters agree that ἄνωθεν is most accurately translated as "from above," as opposed to "from the beginning" or "once more"—primarily because, in other John verses (3:31; 19:11, 23), it expresses the idea of "from above." Rudolf Schnackenburg suggests that John's use of the word in 3:31 expands on the meaning in 3:3 and describes "an event which originates in heaven and is brought about by divine forces outside human control." Schnackenburg, *John*, 1:367. C. H. Dodd and other John scholars contend that the evangelist was aware of the ambiguity of the word and used it intentionally to create an opportunity for Nicodemus to misunderstand Jesus' statement. Dodd, *Interpretation of the Fourth Gospel*, 303 n. 2. In this analysis, I use the phrases "rebirth" and "new birth" to convey the collective idea of being "born from above," "born of God," or "born of water and Spirit."

to "see/enter the kingdom of God" (ἰδεῖν/εἰσελθεῖν εἰς τὴν βασιλείαν τοῦ θεοῦ; 3:3, 5).

In this same discourse, when Jesus says to Nicodemus, "What is born of the flesh is flesh, and what is born of the Spirit is spirit" (τὸ γεγεννημένον ἐκ τῆς σαρκὸς σάρξ ἐστιν καὶ τὸ γεγεννημένον ἐκ τοῦ πνεύματος πνεῦμά ἐστιν; 3:6), it becomes clear that the evangelist is distinguishing between two levels of existence. Here, we begin to understand that being "born of God," "born from above," or "born of water and Spirit" involves becoming a new human being, one who must transition from the lower realm of "flesh" (σάρξ) to the higher realm of "Spirit" (πνεῦμά).

Contemporary Interpretations of New Birth in John

Because the evangelist weaves together so many different-but-related motifs to illustrate the complex idea of birth from above, interpreters tend to focus on discrete aspects of its meaning. Some liken it to the concepts of rebirth and regeneration in Gnostic and Hellenistic religions common at the time the Fourth Evangelist was writing. Others cite examples in Judaism that correspond to the Johannine idea of rebirth; these involve the eschatological idea of humans transformed into heavenly beings in a future age, a concept that shows up in Matthew, for example, as "regeneration," "rebirth," or "renewal of all things" (τῇ παλιγγενεσίᾳ; Matt 19:28).[2] A concept similar to rebirth also appears in the early gospel tradition, as evidenced in Synoptic passages such as, "Unless you change and become like children, you will never enter the kingdom of heaven" (Matt 18:3; Mark 10:15; Luke 18:17).[3] Contemporary mainstream commentators, however, tend to interpret the Johannine concept of rebirth—and movement from the earthly to the

---

2. Dodd, *Interpretation of the Fourth Gospel*, 304. As examples of this idea in Judaism, Dodd cites 1 Enoch 25:6 ("Then they will rejoice greatly, and be glad in the Holy One; they will let its fragrance enter their members, and live a long life upon the earth, as thy fathers lived; and in their days no sorrow or sickness or trouble or affliction will touch them"); 2 Baruch 51:5 ("When therefore they see those, over whom they are now exalted, who shall then be exalted and glorified more than they, they shall respectively be transformed, the latter into the splendor of angels..."); and 2 Baruch 51:10 ("For in the heights of that world shall they dwell, and they shall be made like unto the angels, and be made equal to the stars, and they shall be changed into every form they desire, from beauty into loveliness, and from light into the splendor of glory").

3. Barrett, *John*, 170–72. The concept of rebirth, being born of God, or being born of the Spirit occurs not only in John 1:12 and John 3:8, but also in John 11:52 and other NT passages such as 1 Pet 1:3, 23; Titus 3:5; 1 John 2:29; 3:9; 4:7; 5:1, 4, 18.

heavenly realm—primarily in terms of one or more closely-related ideas: 1) becoming a child of God; 2) entering the kingdom of God; 3) receiving eternal life; and 4) attaining salvation.

Becoming a Child of God

Mainstream commentators such as Raymond E. Brown understand the Johannine concept of new birth primarily in terms of divine begetting. Brown explains rebirth first in terms of becoming a child of God: just as someone becomes human and enters the world as a result of being begotten by his father, an individual can only enter the kingdom of God by being "begotten by a heavenly Father." Although the idea of divine begetting was not common in Hebrew Bible theology, Brown points to several sources as background for this notion: the early stages of the OT tradition, which include the idea of the people of Israel as God's first-born, and the post-exilic stage in which certain Israelites were said to be sons of God.[4]

As Brown clarifies, the evangelist likens begetting by God to the outpouring of the Spirit: "if natural life is attributable to God's giving spirit to men, so eternal life begins when God gives His Holy Spirit to men,"[5] and this gift from God suggests the presence of an entirely new spirit within the person. Brown suggests that John may have found a connection between begetting by God and the gift of the spirit in Jub 1:23–25: "I will create in them a holy spirit and I will cleanse them . . . I will be their Father and they shall be my children."[6] Believers familiar with this part of the tradition would have understood that the outpouring of the Spirit would prepare them for entry into the kingdom of God and for becoming children of God.

Brown then likens the contrast between flesh (σάρξ) and spirit (πνεῦμά) in v. 6 of the Nicodemus discourse to the distinction between earthly humans and those who are children of God. Here, the contrast between flesh and spirit is not the same as the Greek separation of body and soul, nor is it a Gnostic dualism between the material and spiritual. Brown reminds us that man as he is physically born into the world is both material *and* spiritual, and he cites Gen 2:7 in clarifying that "the contrast between

---

4. Brown, *John I–XII*, 138.
5. Ibid., 140.
6. Ibid.

flesh and Spirit is that between man as he is . . . and man as Jesus can make him by giving him a holy Spirit."[7]

Entering the Kingdom of God

Rudolf Schnackenburg is one interpreter who understands birth from above primarily as being granted access to the divine and heavenly realm—the kingdom of God. In his view, "from above" (ἄνωθεν) refers to the divine world, the dwelling-place of God, the kingdom of God, the heavenly realm to which Jesus leads the way; in new birth, the individual is transferred to this dwelling-place of God. Schnackenburg points out that the concept of a higher realm as the dwelling-place of God was a familiar construct in Judaism, one that listeners would have readily recognized. Jewish listeners also would have understood the idea of being transformed by the Spirit in order to fulfill the law of God and enter God's kingdom. The fundamental difference between the two realms of existence—σάρξ and πνεῦμά—is what accounts for humans' inability to enter the kingdom of God on their own. As a result of being born of the earth, humans belong to the world of flesh, and the world of spirit constitutes "a different order of being" that is inaccessible to them. Those who are born of flesh are only that, and those who are born of the Spirit are able to enter the higher, divine realm:[8] "earthly man must be born 'from above,' which means in fact being created anew out of the divine spirit of life; he cannot attain to God's heavenly world otherwise."[9] From this perspective, Jesus is a heavenly representative who comes to give those in the earthly realm the power to become "children of God" (1:12) and gain access to the heavenly realm, God's kingdom.[10]

Receiving Eternal Life

Modern scholars often note that the kingdom-of-God concept we are familiar with from the Synoptic gospels is replaced in John by the motif of "eternal life" (ζωὴν αἰώνιον; 3:15, 16). As early as the Prologue, readers learn that "life" is a major theme of the gospel: "in him was life, and

7. Ibid., 140–41.
8. Schnackenburg, *John*, 1:366–72.
9. Ibid., 1:373.
10. Ibid., 1:382.

the life was the light of all people" (ἐν αὐτῷ ζωὴ ἦν, καὶ ἡ ζωὴ ἦν τὸ φῶς τῶν ἀνθρώπων; 1:4). This theme is reinforced throughout the gospel: Jesus is "the life" (11:25; 14:6), "the bread of life" (6:35, 48), the "light of life" (8:12), the "source of living water . . . gushing up to eternal life" (4:10–14; 7:37–38). He "gives life" (5:21), and his words are "spirit and life" (6:63) and the "words of eternal life" (6:68). All of these references paint a picture of eternal life as a type of existence characterized by a "superabundant quality" that is "everlasting in nature."[11]

C. H. Dodd focuses on this motif as it relates to rebirth, arguing that the entire Nicodemus discourse involves "initiation into eternal life." Pointing to the two spheres of existence (σάρξ and πνεῦμα), Dodd argues that the human being must experience rebirth, must pass from the lower realm to the higher realm, in order to receive eternal life—a state of being only possible in the realm of Spirit. In his view, the background for the idea of "rebirth into eternal life" is Christ's coming into the world; it is his incarnation that opens the door and conditions humanity for this passage. Rebirth then, particularly as expressed in the Nicodemus discourse, is directly tied to Jesus' descent and ascent and has its foundation in the Prologue. When readers encounter the idea that new birth involves the movement of humans from the earthly to the heavenly realm, they recall the Prologue's message that "the Word became flesh" (ὁ λόγος σάρξ ἐγένετο; 1:14) and dwelt among humans.[12] Dodd describes the significance of this connection:

> The incarnation of the Logos is, in other terms, the descent of the Son of Man, or heavenly Man, into the lower sphere, the realm of σάρξ. It is the heavenly Man alone who, having descended, ascends to heaven again. His descent and ascent open to men the possibility of receiving eternal life, that is, of ascending to the sphere of πνεῦμά; in other words, the possibility of rebirth. The possibility becomes an actuality for those who have faith in the Son—which is tantamount (in terms of the Prologue) to "receiving the Logos," with the consequent ἐξουσία to be children of God.[13]

In other words, it is Jesus' incarnation, his descent into the realm of flesh (σάρξ) and his subsequent ascent to heaven by way of the resurrection, that paves the way for humans to ascend into the heavenly realm of spirit (πνεῦμά), be born from above, and receive eternal life. To support his

11. Toon, *Born Again*, 29, 31.
12. Dodd, *Interpretation of the Fourth Gospel*, 305–11.
13. Ibid., 305.

interpretation, Dodd looks to allusions in the text, particularly the verse, "And just as Moses lifted up the serpent in the wilderness, so must the Son of Man be lifted up, that whoever believes in him may have eternal life" (3:14–15). First, Dodd points to the similar meaning between "to raise" (ὑψοῦσθαι), used in John 3:14, and "to cause to ascend" (ἀναβαίνειν), used in the early church to refer to the ascension of Christ. Second, Dodd argues that readers of the Septuagint would recognize the serpent from Wisdom 16:5–6 as "the means through which men passed from death to life" and connect the idea of God's deliverance with Jesus' ascension.[14] In addition, Dodd turns to Philo in his interpretation of the serpent as a symbol of Eve's temptation in Genesis:

> . . . for if the mind has been bitten by pleasure, that is by the serpent which was sent to Eve, shall have strength to behold the beauty of temperance, that is to say, the serpent made by Moses in a manner affecting the soul, and to behold God himself through the medium of the serpent, it shall live. Only let it see and contemplate it intellectually.[15]

Philo's interpretation of the serpent as the means though which one can see God suggests to Dodd that it is possible to attain life through seeing or knowing God—and this he connects to the Johannine motifs of eternal life and new birth. Finally, Dodd refers to the *Corpus Hermeticum*, "The Cup or Monad," in which the author says that by dwelling on and observing God's image with the eyes of the heart, it is possible to "find the Path that leads above," have the image become a guide, and be drawn like a magnet to the sight.[16] Through the lens of this hermetic tractate, Dodd interprets the serpent in John 3:14 as a symbol of God's image through which "the mind might be drawn upward to the vision of God which confers eternal life."[17]

Attaining Salvation

Rudolf Bultmann argues that the Fourth Evangelist altered the meaning of "begotten from above" from a source of Semitic origin to the idea of "rebirth," a Hellenistic idea common in the emerging Christian tradition at the

14. Ibid., 306–7.
15. Philo, *Alleg. Interp.* 2 (81), 46.
16. Mead, "The Cup or Monad," *Corpus Hermeticum* IV. 11.
17. Dodd, *Interpretation of the Fourth Gospel*, 306–7.

time. For Bultmann, rebirth is equivalent to salvation, primarily because the evangelist links rebirth to the "kingdom of God" (τὴν βασιλείαν τοῦ θεοῦ; 3:3, 5) which is, in the Synoptic gospels, a common designation for eschatological salvation. Bultmann further claims that John, in describing requirements for entry into the rule of God, would have assumed that, for the Jewish community, participation in the rule of God is identical to salvation.[18]

Bultmann sees humanity in John as enslaved to darkness, blindness, and falsehood, in bondage to sin and death. Verses such as "And this is the judgment, that the light has come into the world, and people loved darkness rather than light because their deeds were evil" (3:19) and "The world ... hates me because I testify against it that its works are evil" (7:7) suggest that humanity has surrendered itself to these forces, turning away from the light, remaining indifferent to the truth, and rebelling against God. As Bultmann interprets John, because humanity shuts itself off from God and "perverts the creation into the 'world'"—remaining blind to its state of separation and darkness (1:5; 12:46), death (5:19–27), sin (8:21, 34), slavery (8:34–36), and falsehood (8:37, 44)—it is thereby excluded from salvation.[19]

Yet, at the same time Bultmann characterizes the human condition in the Fourth Gospel as one of sinfulness and total exclusion from God's sphere, he also claims that John hints at the possibility of salvation. Bultmann interprets the verse, "No one can see the kingdom of God without being born from above" (3:3) as both stating the impossibility of salvation for humankind and, at the same time, the possibility. In Bultmann's view, a human being can receive salvation only if he can become a totally new person by being "reborn," experiencing birth from above.[20]

While it is helpful to look at the different emphases of various interpreters, all of these ideas are intricately connected and cannot be understood in isolation from one another. Even as an interpreter like Schnackenburg explains new birth in terms of entry into the kingdom of God, he also relates it to eternal life and salvation—claiming that new birth offers access to the divine life and is the "first step toward salvation," a basic requirement for attaining salvation.[21] While a scholar like Brown may focus on rebirth primarily as divine begetting, he sees the concept as closely related to the

18. Bultmann, *John*, 134, 135 n. 2; 135–36 n. 4.
19. Bultmann, *Theology*, 2:26–28.
20. Bultmann, *John*, 133–38.
21. Schnackenburg, *John*, 1:369–74, 379.

ideas of eternal life and the kingdom of God: in his view, it is only when one "is begotten by a heavenly Father" that he is able to enter the kingdom, and "eternal life begins when God gives His Holy Spirit to men"—a begetting through Spirit.[22]

The circular nature of these interpretative claims illustrates the complexity of Johannine thought, the intricacy of the concept of birth from above, and its foundational role in the Fourth Evangelist's theology. These readings also demonstrate the earlier assertion that the interpretive methods we choose determine the questions we are able to ask about a particular text. Not surprisingly, these mainstream (European) scholars have tended to favor interpretations based on the traditional historical-critical method, turning to earlier sources the evangelist might have employed or imagining how John's first audience may have understood the text. These interpretations are important, however, for providing a foundation and context for exploring alternative meaning for readers today.

How Is One "Born from Above?"

Much of contemporary mainstream scholarship has focused primarily on the meaning of John's idea of rebirth, as opposed to the process by which it occurs—the *what* as opposed to the *how*—not surprising, since the evangelist reveals little about how a believer transitions from the earthly realm to the heavenly realm. Interpreters do, however, address the question of whether humans can bring about rebirth through their own actions or whether it can only be effected by God's divine initiative.

Divine Initiative or Human Response?

The text itself suggests strongly that humans do not come to belief entirely through their own effort, that being born from above cannot be achieved by human initiative. When Jesus responds to the disciples' difficulty in understanding his teaching, "For this reason I have told you that no one can come to me unless it is granted by the Father" (6:65), there is the implication that belief and "coming to Jesus," even though they are human actions, depend entirely on God's giving. It is logical, then, to think of rebirth in the same way.

22. Brown, *John I–XII*, 138, 140.

Earlier mainstream interpreters tend to understand new birth this way, mainly in terms of divine action, a miraculous, external event brought about by God and bestowed upon the believer.[23] Scholars such as Johannes Nissen see rebirth as "the result of a divine miracle and not an improvement of the inner nature of man"; others such as C. K. Barrett support the idea of rebirth as "supernatural begetting."[24] Similarly, because the evangelist uses the phrase "born from above" (γεννηθῇ ἄνωθεν; 3:3, 7) in conjunction with "born of water and Spirit" (γεννηθῇ ἐξ ὕδατος καὶ πνεύματος; 3:5), Bultmann makes the case for rebirth being the result of a miraculous event brought about by the Holy Spirit.[25] For him, the word "pneuma" (πνεῦμα) comprises two dimensions: "the miraculous, of that which lies beyond human sphere" and "an event worked in man." In his view, the miraculous event that realizes an individual's potential for becoming πνεῦμα (Spirit) is an encounter with the Revealer:

> In an encounter with the Revealer man is put in question in such a way that his whole past, which determines his present being, is also put in question. Only so can he be called to rebirth, to the rebirth which is the exchange of his old origin, for a new one.[26]

This claim seems to contradict Bultmann's well-known "dualism of decision"—the idea that humans have the ability to choose between two different possibilities for existence—the first being the world of "flesh" (σάρξ), the "this-world" or earthly realm in which life is equivalent to "nothingness," and the second being the world of "spirit" (πνεῦμα), the other-world of divine existence in which humans escape nothingness and experience authentic living. Although Bultmann refers to humanity standing between these two alternatives as a "dualism of decision," he does not propose that humans are free to choose one option over the other; the alternatives are determined by destiny rather than choice. Instead, rebirth is a phenomenon that humans cannot effect on their own, something impossible in the human sphere. From this perspective, rebirth results in eschatological existence, so it can only be the result of divine giving, in which the human

---

23. Howard-Brook, *Becoming Children of God*, 88.
24. Nissen, *John*, 57; Barrett, *John*, 172.
25. Bultmann, *John*, 138–39, 141.
26. Ibid., 159.

"in his whole being from its very origin must be changed into a miraculous, other-worldly being."[27]

Similarly, Schnackenburg interprets the phrase γεννηθῇ ἄνωθεν ("born from above"; 3:3, 7) as "being created anew out of the divine spirit of life."[28] From this perspective, new birth is an event in which an individual is made a new being and given a new way of life. Schnackenburg understands John's concern as God's acting upon the human, an act of God's grace, rather than what the person does or does not do to become a child of God. It is God who makes a new way of life possible for humans by creating in them the foundation for a new being. In the Hebrew tradition, the Holy Spirit was believed to effect "an inward change of heart," a development that would make the individual ready to fulfill the law of God. Schnackenburg reads the evangelist's concept of rebirth as analogous to the idea in the Hebrew tradition of a new creation brought about by God's Spirit. He argues that new birth suggests the need to be "cleansed and totally transformed by God" in order to reach the kingdom of God, and he relates this idea—a creation made new by the power of the Spirit—to the idea of divine adoption

---

27. Bultmann, *John*, 141–42; Bultmann, *Theology*, 2:21. What determines one's potential for achieving salvation and "other-worldly" mode of existence, according to Bultmann, is one's origin. Just as Jesus has his origin in the divine realm of the Father, an individual's destiny is pre-determined by his anthropological origin in the world of the flesh, governing the quality of his life and the person he has been. In order to be "reborn" and achieve salvation, an individual must begin from a completely different starting point and must be able to receive a new origin that will then allow for his salvation. The possibility for salvation depends on one becoming another person altogether; rebirth is "something more than an improvement in man; it means that man receives a new origin." Bultmann, *John*, 135–38, 141. Jeffrey A. Trumbower, in the first full-blown study of anthropology in John's gospel, takes up Bultmann's claim about origin, arguing at length that believers have a "fixed" origin, predetermined before the coming of Jesus; he claims that the evangelist describes an "impenetrable wall" between those who are born from above and those who are from below. Trumbower claims that there is a "pre-salvation affinity" between believers and the divine, arguing for the existence before the coming of Jesus of a distinct group of humans destined to be saved because of their origin. Salvation is not automatic, however; believers need to receive and be given spiritual sight and be transferred from this realm to a higher one. Both Bultmann's and Trumbower's views are counter to those of ancient interpreters such as Paul, Augustine, Luther, and Calvin—for whom all humans in John begin with the same origin and those who are "saved" experience a fundamental change effected by the grace of God. Trumbower, *Born from Above*, 141–45.

28. Schnackenburg, *John*, 1:373.

in the Hebrew tradition and the concept of purification and "inward transformation" in the Qumran community.[29]

For more recent interpreters, however, new birth in John's gospel is the result of human response to God's initiative, and it is this that brings about a change within the believer.[30] Throughout the gospel, the evangelist makes it clear that faith is the expected response of all believers; the call for individuals to believe (πιστεύειν) appears in almost every chapter of John. The evangelist also uses numerous phrases symbolically parallel to believing in order to express the ideal human response to Jesus—"believing," "seeing," "hearing," "listening," "remembering," "keeping," "receiving," "following," "abiding," "dwelling," "knowing," "serving," "worshipping," and "confessing"—all of which suggest different avenues through which individuals come to understand the truth about who Jesus is and what he says. Each of these ideas suggests only one dimension of human response, and they intersect, interconnect, and build on one another to collectively express the complex dynamic involved in choosing the life Jesus offers.[31]

In addition, the underlying purpose of the Fourth Gospel is expressed directly in the closing verses of ch. 20: "these are written so that you may come to believe that Jesus is the Messiah, the Son of God, and that through believing you may have life in his name" (20:31). The human response to Jesus in John can be understood as fully accepting the gift of eternal life Jesus offers, rejecting Jesus and the gift he offers, or standing somewhere along the path toward acceptance.[32] John sees faith as more than simply a matter of belief or unbelief—although he frequently uses those terms—but rather as a continuum along which individuals move as they accept the revelation of God in Jesus.

Several contemporary scholars contend that the distinction between believing/accepting Jesus and rejecting him is primary in John, suggesting that decision *is* an important dimension of believing. John Painter, for example, points to the distinction in John's gospel between believing/unbelieving or accepting/rejecting Jesus, defining unbelief as a rejection of the person of Jesus and what he came to offer. Painter calls attention to what the evangelist describes as problems with believing: false love—such as love of darkness, love of the glory of man, and love of one's own life—or superficial

---

29. Ibid., 1:367–68, 370.
30. Howard-Brook, *Becoming Children of God*, 88.
31. Painter, "Eschatological Faith," 38–41.
32. Reinhartz, *Befriending the Beloved Disciple*, 65.

faith, such as believing in signs. For Painter, authentic faith in John's gospel—especially as attributed to characters such as Nathanael (1:49), Martha (11:27), and Peter (6:68)—is easily distinguishable from superficial faith.[33]

Increasingly, scholars argue for the importance of both divine initiative and human response, that it is within the very act of believing, *choosing* to believe, that divine initiative occurs: "The Father's calling and drawing ... does not precede the decision of faith, but occurs in that decision. Faith is the surrender of self to the calling of God."[34] Even for scholars like Bultmann, who argue for a "pre-determined origin," the process of transferring into the new mode of existence involves believing in the revelation Jesus brings; the Father demands faith and to those who believe, he offers eternal life. Believers who have seen the need for rebirth, who have questioned their previous existence, who have understood Jesus' origins in heaven and his mission as salvation—these are the ones who will receive his revelation in full. It is faith in Jesus' mission that promises life; in contrast, unbelief is cutting oneself off from God's love. Bultmann makes it clear that "faith and unbelief are the answer to the question of the divine love," and belief is an act of responsibility rather than an achievement.[35] Similarly, Leander Keck conflates the ideas of destiny and choice, arguing that how someone responds to Jesus determines his destiny—but if one responds positively to Jesus, his origin and destiny are altered.[36]

Individual Transformation or Communal Change?

Scholarship is divided on the question of whether rebirth in John's Gospel refers to an inner, individual transformation that results in a new kind of living—or an outer, communal act that results in a renewal of the society. The text of John is not entirely clear on this matter. On one hand, a great deal of the stories throughout John feature encounters between Jesus and individual believers but, on the other hand, a message of unity pervades key images such as the Shepherd and his flock or the vine and the branches. Even the Nicodemus passage is perplexing in this regard. It begins with a description of one man (ἄνθρωπος), an identifiable person with an individual and group identity (a Pharisee and a ruler) in dialogue with Jesus.

33. Painter, "Eschatological Faith," 42, 44–49.
34. Culpepper, "Inclusivism and Exclusivism, 96; Bultmann, *Theology*, 2:21–23.
35. Bultmann, *John*, 145, 149–59.
36. Keck, "Derivation as Destiny," 281–82.

He bears the characteristics of a single religious seeker—he comes by night/ darkness (νύξ), suggesting a lack of understanding, and he addresses Jesus as "master" (Ραββεί), indicating his seeking after the truth (3:2).[37] Yet, when he addresses Jesus in the plural ("we know," οἴδαμεν; 3:2), Jesus does the same ("you people must be born again," ὑμᾶς γεννηθῆναι ἄνωθεν; 3:7). As the dialogue expands to encompass more than just Nicodemus ("people loved darkness rather than light," οἱ ἄνθρωποι μᾶλλον τὸ σκότος ἢ τὸ φῶς; 3:19), it ends with a global message that all who love darkness must come into the light (3:21). Is Nicodemus a symbol of an individual man or a communal figure who stands for all of humankind?

Not surprisingly, early contemporary interpreters tend toward more "spiritual" readings that understand the Johannine concept of new birth as a radical and individual transformation of the human person. Bultmann, for example, sees Nicodemus as representing an individual in search of salvation, with the possibility of becoming another person, "a new man" in his encounter with the Revealer. Drawing from the idea of "being like a new-born child" found in Rabbinic Judaism, Bultmann claims that rebirth involves becoming remade into a completely "new creature" on an individual level.[38]

If rebirth in John is equivalent to salvation, then Moule's argument for an "explicitly individualistic type of eschatology" in John bears consideration. As evidence that salvation in John is realized at the level of the individual, Moule cites John 14:21–23, in which Jesus tells the disciples that he will reveal himself to those who love him. When Judas asks why Jesus will reveal himself only to the disciples and not the world, his response is a message about mutual indwelling of Christ and God and the disciples: "Those who love me will keep my word, and my Father will love them, and we will come to them and make our home with them" (14:23). In Moule's view:

> . . . insofar as there is any "coming" to be realized in the near future, it is essentially not a world-wide manifestation but a secret, private coming to each individual as he realizes the fact of the resurrection, loves God in Christ, and accepts him.[39]

---

37. Nissen, *John*, 43–44.
38. Bultmann, *John*, 135–37.
39. Moule, "Individualism of the Fourth Gospel," 172–73.

28   LOVE, LOSS, AND ABJECTION

Moule contends that even if John's gospel has dimensions that relate to the people of God as a community, its real depth rests in its exploration of the individual's affinity with God, "the meaning of individual relations with God in Christ."[40]

Because there is no precedent in Hebrew Scripture for the idea of individual rebirth or renewal, scholars look to other sources to support this interpretation. Dodd and Barrett, for example, support the notion of individual rebirth with the *Corpus Hermeticum* tractate XIII, "On Rebirth"[41] (a document written after John), arguing that the idea of *individual* renewal was part of the background of thought from which the evangelist drew. Schnackenburg also highlights the emphasis in Judaism, in the apocrypha and rabbinical writings, on the Holy Spirit whose function was to effect "an inner change of heart" in man.[42] Traditionally, John's gospel has been read in this way, understanding the human person who is born from above as being transformed at the very level of being, an inner transformation that is essentially an individual experience.[43]

More recent scholarship favors a "social reading," understanding John's rebirth theme in terms of communal change. Throughout the text, there is a call for believers to become involved in community. Andrew reaches out to his brother, Peter (1:35–42), Philip goes to Nathanael (1:43–46), and the Samaritan woman goes out to residents of her city (4:28–30). The notion of keeping Jesus' commandment also extends outward; when Jesus says "If you love me, you will keep my commandments" (14:15), the Johannine concept of abiding with Jesus is not a personal, inner dimension of belief but an outward focus on the importance of love for others. This need for mutual love arises naturally because, as those who believe in Jesus continue to do his works, they will be persecuted and may face the possibility of giving their lives for each other—"to lay down one's life for one's friends" (15:12–13).

40. Ibid., 182.

41. One of the 17 Hermetic tractates written in Egypt between the second and fifth centuries CE, "On Rebirth" bears striking similarities to John's concept of new birth, not in language but in content. In the dialogue on rebirth, readers learn that no one is "able to be saved before regeneration" (v. 1) and that "the son of God, the one Man" is the author of regeneration (v. 4). The dialogue also describes the manner of rebirth: when one has "become alienated from the world" (v. 1), has strengthened one's mind "away from the world's deception" (v. 1), has come out of one's self "into an immortal body" (v. 3), and when "twelve punishments of matter ... depart" (v. 7). Grese, *Corpus Hermeticum XIII*, 1–15.

42. Schnackenburg, *John*, 1:370.

43. Rensberger, *Johannine Faith*, 79; Brodie, *John*, 38.

Keeping Jesus' commandment, in this case, means not only demonstrating affection and kindness toward one another but also standing in solidarity with other believers against the outside world.[44]

David Rensberger is one interpreter who argues for Nicodemus as a communal symbol, claiming that becoming a true believer also results in becoming part of the community of those who believe in Jesus, dissolving connections with established social structures that once had meaning, and committing one's loyalties to the new group. Rensberger would argue for the focus of John 3 to be not rebirth itself, but the kingdom into which a community is rebirthed.[45] Similarly, Johannes Nissen points out that the "kingdom of God"—closely allied in John to the idea of rebirth—is a social category that, since it occurs so rarely in John, the evangelist must have retained intentionally from an earlier tradition in order to communicate the social dimension of salvation. In this view, to be born from above, to pass from one world to the other is not only to become part of a new community, but also to experience a reorientation of the entire community, one "so profound and far-reaching as to be a new birth."[46]

Not surprisingly, scholars increasingly are reading the concept of born from above in John's gospel as signifying both a personal and communal transformation. Gail R. O'Day interprets birth from above as receiving a new identity as a child of God and a new community, and in this community one has the opportunity to be a part of a renewed family formed of those who also have become children of God: "Thus, through belief in Jesus' name, *we* become a new people and *I* become a new person."[47]

---

44. Brodie, *John*, 37.

45. Rensberger, *Johannine Faith*, 38–40, 55–56. Rensberger draws on the historical context of the Johannine community to support his claim that Nicodemus should be understood as a symbol of communal and social unity. He argues that Nicodemus is depicted as someone with inadequate faith and commitment, and his function is to represent a group that the evangelist wants to paint in this light—the secret Christian Jews or "crypto-Christians" that were a reality in the world of the Johannine community. Members of this group were willing to acknowledge Jesus as a miracle-worker and divinely-sent teacher but nothing more. For this reason, Rensberger argues, the evangelist used the Nicodemus discourse to highlight the importance of taking action to break old ties and loyalties and to become fully a member of the Johannine Christian group. Regardless of whether the text represents the experience of the Johannine community itself, many contemporary scholars agree that it expresses a call to leave behind the "revelation-rejecting world" and join the community of believers. Brodie, *John*, 39.

46. Nissen, "Rebirth and Community," 131–32.

47. O'Day, "New Birth as a New People," 53.

Present Reality or Future Vision?

Not only is there ambiguity in John as to *how* one is born from above—whether it results from divine initiative or human effort, whether it is an individual or communal transformation—there also is ambiguity around the question of *when* it occurs—now or in the age to come. The text seems to suggest both: the first few verses of the Nicodemus discourse (3:2–8) tell us that being born from above is required in order to enter the kingdom of God. The following verses (3:9–21), however, make it clear that being born from above *only* is possible when the Son is lifted up, that is, only through Jesus' death, resurrection, and ascension.[48]

Barrett sees the kingdom of God and the experience of being reborn first and foremost as operative in the here and now of the gospel story. Because the Fourth Evangelist depicts the kingdom of God as already present in Jesus, and because he "is the one who baptizes with the Holy Spirit" (1:33), Barrett sees the disciples in John as already having experienced the new reality; they, in fact, are "a stage nearer to seeing and entering the kingdom of God."[49] But Barrett also points out how the evangelist adapted existing parallel ideas—the notion of the kingdom of God and the idea of an eschatological transformation in the age to come, both from Orthodox Judaism, as well as regeneration from the Hellenistic context—and gave them "an exceptionally urgent apocalyptic note." The Fourth Evangelist adapts these concepts from an idea of a metaphysical miracle far off in the future, to a possibility for a religiously significant event—entering the kingdom of God—that happens here and now. In this way, the author of John arrived at a unique and paradoxical depiction of "two moments" in Christian life: the kingdom already present and the kingdom fully consummated at Jesus' resurrection and ascension.[50]

Barrett point outs that John did not plagiarize the exact idea of regeneration from the Hellenistic context, nor did he imitate the kingdom of God idea from the language of Judaism. Instead, he used the two terms to express something entirely new, something that was not Hellenistic or Jewish but uniquely Christian:[51]

---

48. Nissen, *John*, 45.
49. Barrett, *John*, 169.
50. Ibid., 172.
51. Ibid., 170–72.

He set out from an exceptionally clear perception of the two "moments" of Christian salvation, that of the work accomplished and that of the work yet to be consummated; and he perceived that the language of Judaism (the kingdom of God) and the language of Hellenism (γεννηθῆναι ἄνωθεν) provided him with a unique opportunity of expressing what was neither Jewish nor Hellenistic but simply Christian.[52]

Barrett's explanation of John's "two moments" of salvation suggests that a transformation occurs at two points in a believer's life: a spiritual rebirth, in which believers are given "the present experience of eternal life" in the here and now—and a physical/bodily restoration, when believers will be "raised up in the last day."[53]

Seeking a New Model for Johannine Rebirth

Existing Models for Understanding Rebirth

While the text of John reveals little about how one is born from above, recent interpreters have attempted to describe the process of rebirth by

---

52. Ibid., 173.

53 Ladd, *Theology of the New Testament*, 294. J. Louis Martyn and Raymond E. Brown's understanding of a "two-level drama" in John also bears on the distinction between these two moments. Martyn and Brown's contention, that the text relates two parallel stories—one a story about Jesus and the events of his time and, the other a depiction of the events occurring to the Johannine community of the author's time—helps explain the ambiguity in the text itself about whether rebirth or renewal occurs in the here and now or at a future time. The evangelist, writing in a time when the Johannine community had come to believe in the resurrection and glorification of Jesus, reflects in the text the idea that the age of the Spirit and birth from above will occur after this event. Martyn, *History and Theology*, 47. Several scholars dispute Martyn and Brown's claims, however. Wayne Meeks, for example, counters Martyn's "two-level drama," specifically his contention that the text of John refers to expulsion from the synagogue (ἀποσυνάγωγος)—particularly 9:22b, ". . . for the Jews had already agreed that anyone who confessed Jesus to be the Messiah would be put out of the synagogue." Meeks argues that there is no textual or historical evidence for Martyn's theory that this verse refers to the reformulation of the Twelfth Benediction, which Christians would not have been able to recite in the synagogue service. Meeks, "Breaking Away," 102. Tobias Hägerland also disputes the two-level drama, arguing that not only is there no historical precedent in the author's time of a genre meant to be read on two levels, but also there are no textual clues to suggest it. He, too, dismisses text references to expulsion from the synagogue (ἀποσυνάγωγος), claiming that there occurred numerous ongoing expulsions and persecutions even during Jesus' time. Hägerland, "John's Gospel," 309–22.

bringing to bear the tools of literary criticism, by applying a theological perspective, or by analyzing the text through a psychological lens.

Literary Models

Several interpreters have used literary analysis to examine the movement of characters in the narrative. These literary models also have proved useful for understanding the process of transformation that believers experience in John's gospel as they accept who Jesus is, receive his offer of eternal life, and become children of God. Dorothy Lee calls on form criticism to analyze the patterns of characters' progress through the faith journey, and she identifies five stages: 1) a miraculous happening/sign-event (σημεῖον) such as a healing or a feeding; 2) a literal/mistaken understanding; 3) a struggle to grasp meaning; 4) an acceptance/rejection of Jesus as the one sent from God; and 5) a statement of faith/commitment to discipleship or a statement of rejection. Lee analyzes six narrative passages in John's gospel, and in each of them, she traces the character's movement in the journey of either coming to accept Jesus or reject him. She cites the Nicodemus discourse as an example of a narrative in which the character does *not* advance to a statement of faith or commitment to discipleship. In this discourse, Lee claims that the image of birth from above is a symbol of eternal life (and therefore like a sign-event). In response to Jesus' statement about birth from above, Nicodemus interprets it literally, misunderstanding the symbolic/ metaphorical import, and missing Jesus' meaning entirely. Finally, although Jesus reveals himself as the descending Son of Man, Nicodemus is unwilling to make an authentic response of faith; he is not able to experience the reorientation or creative new beginning to become one of God's children.[54] Lee's notion of the progress of transformation in John's gospel is instructive in that it acknowledges the role of conflict or struggle in believers' lives, as well as the presence of a miraculous event or sign of divine initiative. Yet, her reading limits the transformation of a believer to the level of intellectual understanding and knowledge.

---

54. Lee, *Symbolic Narratives*, 11–15, 61–63.

Theological Models

Others seek to explain the change that believers undergo in John through the lens of theology—framing a series of stages in theological terms. One such theological model, proposed by Thomas Brodie, highlights several phases of spiritual development, particularly as illustrated in the events depicted in ch. 13-17. He identifies in these chapters a three-stage divine initiative—manifest in Jesus—that takes three basic forms: cleansing, purifying, and sanctifying. The *cleansing* aspect Brodie sees at work in Jesus' washing of the disciples' feet: "Jesus said to him, 'One who has bathed does not need to wash, except for the feet, but is entirely clean'" (13:10). Brodie compares the pruning of the vines by the vinegrower in ch. 15 to the idea of *purifying*: "Every branch that bears fruit he prunes to make it bear more fruit" (15:2). And he finds the final form of divine initiative, *sanctifying*, in Jesus' prayer to make the disciples holy: "Sanctify them in the truth; your word is truth" (17:17)—sometimes referred to as "The Consecration Prayer." Brodie applies his concept of a three-fold divine initiative to the community of disciples as a whole and to the larger narrative arc of the gospel. He interprets the overarching divine movement, enacted by Jesus but ultimately the work of God, as carrying "the believer into the realm of the spirit."[55]

In Brodie's model, this three-stage divine initiative moves the individual believer into unity with the community. In response to the divine initiative, believers experience first a greater sense of cleanliness and purity, then a growing insight or awareness of the divine presence, and finally a union of the divine and human. As an example of this transformation, Brodie points to the verse at the close of ch. 14, "Rise, let us be on our way" (14:31), considered by most scholars to be an aporia that signals the patching together of material from various sources. Brodie counters traditional thinking, reading the verse as intentional, John's way of "inviting the believers to leave a previous situation and to rise to a new level."[56] He sees believers as being prompted to advance, to place their eyes on God, and to leave the past behind, a "departure and arrival" he sees as essential to the spiritual journey the disciples are making.[57] Although Brodie's reading illuminates the divine initiative depicted in the John text, it relegates the

---

55. Brodie, *John*, 430-31.
56. Ibid., 437.
57. Ibid.

human response to passive acceptance of God's transforming power. In the absence of conflict or struggle, there is no precipitating event to prompt a change in the believer or in which the believer may participate.

Psychological Models

Several scholars have employed a psychological lens to interpret transformative faith in John's gospel, a phenomenon akin to rebirth. Paul N. Anderson, for example, calls attention to the transformative nature of Jesus' actions and mission, the impact of his radically new and original teachings, and argues for the importance of considering not only *what* Jesus taught but also *how* he taught. In his analysis, Anderson looks at Jesus' approaches from the perspective of cognitive dissonance theory, which argues that "where contradictions are perceived between one's self-conceptions and one's behaviors, or perhaps between two competing self-perceptions, one is driven to reconcile the discrepancies and move toward a more consonant self-conception."[58] In this view, Jesus comes to provoke, to create crisis, and to introduce dissonance—by his association with John the Baptist, his cleansing of the Temple, his healing of the sick on the Sabbath, his dining with sinners and tax collectors, and his references to God as his Father. In particular, the Johannine Jesus' claims that the Son is equal to the Father, and that Jesus and the Father are one, would be provocative enough to transform believers' thinking. All of these actions, according to Anderson, are intended to disturb the comfortable and prompt believers to move out of their accustomed ways of thinking and experience a transformation to more advanced levels of thinking and perceiving.[59] While I agree with Anderson's claim about Jesus creating cognitive dissonance, the change engendered by such an event is intellectual and not necessarily transformative.

Anderson also attempts to apply to John theories of faith development, particularly J. Loder's understanding of spiritual encounters—in an attempt to understand "knowing as a transforming event." Loder identifies five stages that are part of any spiritual transformation or epistemological change: 1) a sense of conflict with a current experience or situation; 2) a period of seeking solutions to the conflict; 3) imaginatively constructing a tentative solution to the conflict; 4) simultaneously releasing the conflict and opening to moving beyond previously-held notions of truth; and 5)

58. Anderson, "Jesus and Transformation," 308.
59. Ibid., 306–20.

reflecting back on the meaning of the event and interpreting the implications for the future.[60] This idea gets closer to describing the kind of change represented by the Johannine idea of new birth—but can "knowing" really be a transformative event? This model suggests an epistemological rupture (at best) or a change in perception (at least)—neither of which signify the kind of change being expressed by John's notion of birth from above.

In deconstructing the process of new birth, these models provide a deeper look at the transformation hinted at by the Johannine Jesus. What they lack, however, is an exploration of the dynamic interplay in John between the divine initiative and human response—the why and how of God, through Jesus, effecting transformation in certain individuals as opposed to others. The limitations of these models prevent them from providing a comprehensive explanation of birth from above; they also fail to offer an understanding that can move beyond the text itself to inform the lives of readers today.

A Proposed Psychoanalytic Approach

By exploring these interpretations of new birth in John's gospel, I seek to identify a more useful model for understanding the process—one that brings together both the divine initiative and human response, both individual transformation and community change, and both the present reality and a future vision. This study proposes an alternative framework for understanding the meaning of Johannine rebirth, one based on psychoanalytic theories about the development of human selfhood. What does psychoanalytic theory have to do with rebirth? In addition to exploring the initial "birth" of the self in infancy, psychoanalytic theory also investigates influences on the development of an individual's selfhood over the lifespan.

Central to this study are the theories of Julia Kristeva, a thinker known for her work not only in psychoanalytic theory but also in philosophy, linguistics and language theory, literary criticism, and culture. It is precisely Kristeva's cross-disciplinary approach that makes her thinking profoundly original and complex and, while it is impossible to untangle the various dimensions of Kristeva's thought, this study primarily calls upon her work in psychoanalytic theory.

Along with other post-structuralists, Kristeva breaks away from the Western philosophic tradition (aligning herself with philosophers such as

---

60. Anderson, *Christology of the Fourth Gospel*, 148–50.

Hegel and Nietzsche), arguing against the idea of the self as a "unified and rational being." Conventional understandings of subjectivity conceive of the human self as being in control, guided by reason, and fully conscious of one's desires, intentions, and actions. But, for Kristeva and her colleagues, individuals are not stable entities or "selves," but "subjects" profoundly influenced by a variety of phenomena such as culture, language, and history, influences over which they have no control. Kristeva's use of the term "subjectivity" is meant to convey the idea that human development is a complex process by which individuals are "subject" to and shaped by invisible forces of which they are largely unaware.[61]

She also insists on a dynamic, process-oriented understanding of human subjectivity—the means by which an individual becomes a self. In her view, each human person is always in the process of becoming, individuals whose subjectivity is never finally determined; they are continuously being formed as subjects, constantly shaped by the environment. Becoming a self or "subject," in Kristeva's view, then is a dynamic process that is ongoing throughout one's life; it is not something that occurs just at birth. Human beings are constituted through a variety of processes, events, experiences, and exchanges.

Kristeva advances her theory of how a human being's selfhood initially takes shape in infancy by building on the work of psychoanalysts Sigmund Freud and Jacques Lacan. All three of these theorists explore the beginnings of subjectivity in a developing child's relationship with its parents, but each identifies a different precipitating event in the life of the child.

For Freud, the infant begins life in a realm of plenitude, not yet able to distinguish between itself (inside) and mother (outside); in this imaginary space separate from the outer world, the developing child first experiences its mother, who satisfies the infant's natural needs for self-preservation. Some of the child's needs, however, go beyond mere biological drives and involve the attainment of enjoyment—what Freud refers to as the "pleasure principle" and describes as "a relaxation of . . . tension . . . avoidance of pain or . . . production of pleasure."[62] One example is the child's feeding at the mother's breast; even as the infant's physical needs for nourishment are satisfied, she may continue to try to obtain pleasure from sucking. In Freud's view, a pivotal point in the child's development occurs when the "reality principle" intrudes, disrupting the mother/child connection and

---

61. McAfee, *Julia Kristeva*, 1–2, 6–7.
62. Freud, *Beyond the Pleasure Principle*, 1.

placing limitations on the infant's pleasure-seeking drives. As the external world breaks into the realm of plenitude the infant enjoys with the mother, the child's self begins to take shape as she negotiates the balance between unconscious inner desires and the demands of external reality.[63]

Freud sees this ongoing tension between the pleasure principle and the reality principle as constitutive of human selfhood and life. As the developing infant encounters people and objects in the external world, she unconsciously selects, identifies, and incorporates them into herself, and it is this identification and incorporation that creates the foundation and structure of the self. Essential to this process, however, is a sense of loss, because it is the loss of a loved one that prompts the child to take in that person into the structure of the self and "attempt to *become* like the lost love."[64]

Freud's contention that the development of the human self emerges from feelings of loss leads to his well-known theory of the Oedipus complex. As the child becomes aware of what the father has and the mother lacks—not only the phallus but also the power it represents—this prompts a different cycle of response in male and female subjects. Freud sees the male child as first desiring sexual union with his mother; as his fantasy is disrupted by the father, the boy then comes to hate and fear the father; finally, out of an imagined threat of castration, the boy is forced to give up his desire for the mother, turning away from her toward the father. For the girl child, it is the discovery of what she lacks that leads her to conclude that she has been castrated; she assumes her mother also has been, so she also turns away from the mother toward the father. Freud proposes that this fear of castration in the developing male child and envy of power in the female child is essential for the formation of identity and for the child's entry into the social order.[65]

In theorizing the emergence of selfhood/subjectivity, Freud's interests tend to center on the bodily, natural, or neurological conditions of human development, while Lacan emphasizes the ideological structures by which humans come to understand their relationships with others. Both theorists agree that the infant child exists initially in a symbiotic relationship with the maternal body, a dyadic union Freud characterizes as a plenitude. Lacan calls this state "the imaginary," and he characterizes it as a merging of

---

63. Freud, *Beyond the Pleasure Principle*, 1–7; Elliott, *Psychoanalytic Theory*, 18–22.
64. Elliott, *Psychoanalytic Theory*, 20–22.
65. Ibid., 21–22.

internal and external, a "realm of ideal completeness" that forms the foundation for development of selfhood and identity.[66]

In Lacan's construct, the starting point for the formation of subjectivity is the "mirror stage" between the ages of six and eighteen months, when the child becomes fascinated with its own reflection and begins to be aware of the body as a separate form. While the image can be confusing at first, eventually the child comes to identify with it and recognizes that self as "I," a subject separate from others. Although Lacan insists that image in the mirror is a distortion—an "ideal I" as opposed to an accurate reflection—nevertheless, subjectivity begins to take shape as the child gains a sense of self-unity.[67]

Around the same time, Lacan sees the developing child turning toward the father, but not in the way Freud theorizes. In response to Freud's focus on envy or fear related to the phallus, Lacan underscores that the male organ is a signifier of power and sexual difference: "what women lack and what men have." The child desires what the phallus *represents*, and this Lacan terms *nom-du-père* ("Law of the Father"). But, because it is a symbol, it can never actually be acquired, and the resulting development is desire. In Lacan's view, it is at this point that the child moves into the symbolic realm, beginning to use language to satisfy a desire that can never be met, and the individual is formed as a human subject. In contrast to Freud, Lacan argues that "the father intrudes into the child/mother dyad in a symbolic capacity, as the representative of the wider cultural network . . ."[68]

For Kristeva, the formation of the individual as a subject also relates to a child's separation from the mother, but not in the way Freud proposes. It also occurs earlier than Lacan's mirror stage suggests. Subjectivity—how an individual comes to understand herself or himself as an independent being—arises through the process Kristeva calls "abjection." Before an infant has learned language and before it has become a subject, it dwells in oneness with its mother—what Kristeva calls the "semiotic *chora*." But in order to become a complete and whole being, the child must do the impossible and separate from its mother. The child does so by drawing a boundary between itself and its mother and rejecting everything associated with the maternal body. Bodily elements must be cast out and rejected as vile and

---

66. Ibid., 102–3.
67. Lacan, "The Mirror Stage," 103–4.
68. Elliott, *Psychoanalytic Theory*, 105.

disgusting: blood, vomit, excrement, even sour milk. Abjection, like birth, is a violent separation of one body from another.[69]

As a result of abjection, the child arrives at what Kristeva calls a "mapping of the self's clean and proper body."[70] Contrasting the "clean" body with the abject maternal body allows the child to form identity and boundaries—and everything from this point on that threatens the child's sense of cleanliness and propriety is abject. Ultimately, the child abjects everything that is seen as Other to the newly formed sense of self until, finally, it is "not lack of cleanliness or health that causes abjection but what disturbs identity, system, order . . . what does not respects borders, positions, rules."[71]

Although Kristeva insists that abjection is a necessary step in an infant's separation from the mother, she also makes it clear that it is much more than that; abjection also is something an individual may experience throughout life at moments of extreme crisis, suffering, horror, or taboo. Kristeva's theory of abjection, then, informs our understanding of not only the constructs of Self and Other, but also those of inside/outside, pure/impure, strange/familiar, inclusion/exclusion. She acknowledges that, in much the same way that an individual abjects the mother in order to form a distinct identity, societies, too, abject the feminine. And because Kristeva stresses the maternal body as the prototype for all subjective relations—because its unity is challenged by the Other within (an "Other-in-process")—it also is a model for the "subject-in-process," what Kristeva refers to as *"le sujet en procès."* Each of us is always in the process of becoming, individuals whose subjectivity is never finally determined; we are continuously being shaped and formed as subjects.[72]

Overview of Proposed Model

If we return for a moment to existing models for understanding rebirth in John, we will note that the common thread is an experience of *blindness* or lack of awareness in the life of an individual believer, followed by a *disruption or break* in awareness, resulting in a *dramatic alteration* of the person's perceptions of the world and his or her sense of place in it. Beverly Roberts Gaventa describes this as "a sharp discontinuity . . . that breaks the person's

69. Kristeva, *Powers of Horror*, 1–5; Oliver, "Kristeva's Imaginary Father," 48.
70. Kristeva, *Powers of Horror*, 72.
71. Ibid., 4.
72. McAfee, *Julia Kristeva*, 29–43.

ties to 'this world' and its perceptions."[73] It is this disruption or discontinuity that the evangelist evokes in the juxtaposition of "the world above" and "the world below," the heavenly realm and the earthly realm, life and death, light and darkness, sight and blindness—and believers are called over and over to turn away from the world below, from the darkness, blindness, and death-enslaved ways of "this world" and to turn toward the world above, the divine realm, the world of light and life.

The model I propose as an interpretive lens for understanding rebirth in John's gospel follows a similar pattern—tracing Mary's transition from blindness to disruption to alteration—but is different in several respects. First, because it is grounded in Kristeva's theories of the development of human selfhood, Mary's transformation is not a discrete series of steps; rather it is a continuous movement toward becoming. Second, this proposed model goes beyond the dualism many find in John's gospel; as Mary is transformed, she does not leave the world below for the world above, but becomes more deeply engaged in the world as a newly constituted self. In this way, it has repercussions that are both individual and communal. Third, this model overturns the perceived split between body and spirit, as Mary's transformation shows them existing in healthy tension with one another. Finally, this way of understanding rebirth acknowledges the divine initiative and human response in the process of transformation—and it honors the two "moments" of Christian life—both the present reality of transformation in the here and now while still allowing for a vision of the kingdom in the future.

From Illusion to Disruption: John 11:1–37

Kristeva proposes that a developing infant begins life in a nurturing, protected environment known as the "semiotic *chora*," a state in which she senses herself and her mother as one. At a certain point, the child becomes aware that the mother is not as all-powerful as she imagined, and this realization disrupts the peaceful co-existence of child and mother. It is this awareness that propels the child to turn away from the mother, abjecting her and everything associated with her. Through the lens of Kristeva's theory, I explore how Mary of Bethany exists in a state of false security at the beginning of her story, believing herself to be part of Jesus' inner circle and relying on the knowledge that he surely will help her brother, his friend.

73. Gaventa, *From Darkness to Light*, 135, 138.

Her security is disrupted when her brother dies and, attempting to reject death, she looks to Jesus for help. When he fails to respond, the reality of death breaks into and interrupts the life Mary knows, and she sees that the world is not as she believed it to be.

From Disruption to Recognition: John 11:38–45

In the next stage of Kristeva's developmental theory, the infant has turned away from the mother and left the protection of the semiotic *chora*, and she now exists in a liminal space. Moving from her original narcissistic stance, the child begins to be aware that there is something that is "nother," and she begins to see that there is another world previously unknown to her. This study examines Mary of Bethany's story in light of this stage, particularly what happens to her during Jesus' raising of Lazarus. Although Mary does not act or speak in this segment of the narrative, it is possible to infer a new awareness created in her by the unfolding events and by the in-breaking of the divine into her life. She, too, is in a liminal place as she witnesses the raising of her brother and encounters an alternative reality revealed to her by Jesus.[74]

From Recognition to Participation in the Life of the Divine: John 12:1–8

Kristeva's theory suggests that the developing child, after having separated from her mother, turns toward the father. Transferring her attachment to him, the child is drawn to what he represents—authority, power, and a world beyond what she has previously known. This is the onset of subjectivity, the point at which the child's self and identity begin to take shape. By examining Mary's story from the perspective of this developmental stage, I seek to reveal her new subjectivity—her new identity as a child of God, as an empowered self, and as an individual who has been born from above.

---

74. This proposed model does not equate the developing child's father with Jesus or suggest that the human father represents or is a stand-in for the Divine. In the child's reality, the father represents the broader world and an unknown reality beyond the protected confines of the semiotic *chora*.

2

The World as Illusion

JOHN 11:1–37

Introduction

Biblical scholar Mary Ann Beavis recently noted that there is not a single scholarly monograph or article devoted to exploring the role of Mary of Bethany in her own right. In analyses of Mary's involvement in the few John scenes in which she appears, she has been consistently overshadowed by her sister Martha and, for the better part of Christian history, she has been conflated with either the anonymous sinner in Luke's gospel (Luke 7:36–50) or with Mary Magdalene (John 20:1–23). In no surveys of women in the gospels or of Marys in the biblical tradition is Mary of Bethany found to be a significant figure.[1] Yet, while Mary's appearances in John are brief, a close reading of the narrative indicates a much greater role for her than previously imagined.

In this reading of John, I employ what Mieke Bal calls "counter-coherences"—deconstructive ways of interpreting a text that challenge the repetitive and oppressive narratives that pass for truth. Recognizing the cultural embeddedness of all narratives, Bal's goal is to resist the ideological "slogans" embedded in hegemonic narratives and turn the background of a text into a recognizable foreground. Bal claims that her approach allows for analyzing the relationship between the text and its historical context in a new way, and she calls for openness to unexpected interpretations that

1. Beavis, "Mary of Bethany," 740; Beavis, "Reconsidering," 283.

can account for details in the text that were previously unexplainable. One of her approaches is "focalization," by which she means to distinguish the overtly dominant voice or vision in a text from alternatives that may be possible—reading a text from the point of view of someone other than the narrator or main character.[2] My interpretation of John, instead of focusing on Jesus as the dominant voice or character, uses Bal's counter-coherence approach to foreground Mary of Bethany's life, voice, and experience. This approach allows me to address details in the text that have previously been dismissed and—as I proposed in the Introduction—to explore questions about the story that dominant interpretations have blinded us to, questions whose answers may resonate with a contemporary reader's self-awareness and understanding of Jesus.

We meet Mary and Martha at the midpoint of John's gospel story, when their brother Lazarus is ill. The sisters send word to Jesus, asking him to help his friend ("Lord, he whom you love is ill," 11:3), and the implication is that the women not only are friends of Jesus, but also are well aware of his ability to heal. Instead of rushing directly to the aid of the friends he loves, however, Jesus remains two days longer before going to Bethany. When he does draw near to the village, Jesus discovers that Lazarus has already been dead for four days. Going out to meet him, Martha says to Jesus, "Lord, if you had been here, my brother would not have died" (11:21), but Jesus immediately assures her that Lazarus will rise again. She understands him to be referring to the resurrection on the last day, but he corrects her in responding, "I am the resurrection and the life" (11:25), explaining that all who believe in him will never die. Jesus asks Martha if she believes what he says, and she responds with a complete confession of faith, proclaiming Jesus to be the "Messiah, the Son of God, the one coming into the world" (11:27). Martha then returns home and tells Mary that Jesus is calling for her. Along with the Jewish mourners, Mary goes to meet Jesus and, when she reaches him, kneels at his feet and says exactly the words her sister said earlier, "Lord, if you had been here, my brother would not have died" (11:32). Jesus sees that Mary and her friends are weeping, and he is moved to tears as well. He asks them to lead him to the tomb, and they do so.

Interpreters of this passage most often see Martha as an exemplary disciple, primarily because she responds with the most complete profession of faith in the Gospel so far. Because her confession appears as it does at this climactic phase of Jesus' signs, some scholars suggest that it carries more

2. Bal, *Death and Dissymmetry*, 20–21.

weight than other, similar confessions. Her proclamation is compared to Peter's faith statement in Matthew ("You are the Messiah, the Son of the living God"; Matt 16:16), placing her on equal footing with one of the Twelve, and her status (and Mary's) as someone Jesus loves gives her near-equality with the Beloved Disciple. In addition, Martha's summoning of Mary to come see Jesus (11:28) is likened to Andrew and Philip's invitation to Peter and Nathanael early in Jesus' ministry (1:35–51)—and this suggests that Martha already is among the first disciples when she "calls" Mary to discipleship.[3]

Mary's actions, especially when compared to Martha's intellectual response to Jesus, appear intensely passionate and emotional. Because Mary's role often is not considered as important as Martha's in this passage, she is interpreted as meek and passive; not only does she remain at home while Martha actively seeks to receive Jesus and then goes to him only when Martha summons her, but also she weeps and kneels before him. Next to the self-confident and forthright Martha, Mary appears to some commentators as quiet, tranquil, and worshipful[4] and, to others, she appears to be displaying "an attitude of hopelessness and lack of trust."[5]

As we will see, however, not only does the narrative of John portray Mary as the primary character in every passage in which she appears, but also it offers textual clues that highlight her significance in the larger story. This section of my analysis considers Mary's place in the world of the narrative, her identity and presence, her relationship with Jesus, her encounter with death, and her subsequent grief. The larger structure of this chapter traces Kristeva's theory of how human subjectivity emerges; within that framework, I explore Mary's experiences to follow the arc of her transformation and to reveal insights about the process of being born from above.

The Semiotic Chora

Mary's Role, Her World, and Her Relationship with Jesus

The text is silent on Mary's life prior to her appearance in ch. 11 but, in the very first verse, we learn that she and her sister are significant characters: the village of Lazarus is identified as "the village of Mary and her sister

3. Reinhartz, "From Narrative to History," 174–76.
4. Moltmann-Wendel, *Women around Jesus*, 54–55.
5. Witherington, *Women in the Ministry of Jesus*, 109.

Martha" (11:1). The Fourth Evangelist is known for portraying women in ways that challenge the prevailing ideology of his time, and Mary and Martha are prime examples of John's counter-ideology when it comes to gender. They are Jewish women living independently in Bethany, and there is no indication in the text that they are now or ever have been married. Their participation is not limited to the private sphere of the home, their identities are not defined by participation in marriage or other kinship relations, and they have the freedom to follow Jesus and enjoy a close friendship with him. Mary is signaled as the more important of the two; not only is she mentioned first, but also Martha is named as "her sister" (11:1), and Lazarus is identified as "her brother" (11:2). Even more noteworthy, Mary is referred to as "the one who anointed the Lord with perfume and wiped his feet with her hair" (11:2)—a verse that prompts readers to associate Mary with the unnamed woman in the Synoptic gospels. Through the use of what narrative criticism refers to as "mutual contextual beliefs,"[6] the evangelist invites the reader (or listener) into a world of shared knowledge and alerts us to the fact that Mary is to play a prominent role in the story.

The World Mary Inhabits

At the beginning of Mary's story, we can infer that the world she inhabits is comparatively safe and comfortable. Because she lives with her sister and brother, it is likely that she is secure financially, and the reference to her anointing Jesus in the following chapter suggests that her family may even be well-to-do. Some interpretations suggest that the house in Bethany belongs to the sisters and that they are leaders of a house church.[7] Although Mary's parents presumably have died, her connection with the Judeans indicates that she has a supportive community and perhaps even a network of friends. Her close relationship with Jesus rounds out this picture, providing a strong foundation for her security and giving her special standing in the community.

Mary also has a strong relationship with Jesus; when the sisters send word to Jesus asking him to help their brother, his friend—"Lord, he whom you love is ill" (Κύριε, ἴδε ὃν φιλεῖς ἀσθενεῖ; 11:3)—the narrative makes it clear that not only are the women friends of Jesus, but also they and their brother are "loved" (ἠγάπα) by Jesus; they are, in fact, the only characters

6. Bach and Harnish, *Linguistic Communication and Speech Acts*, 5–6.
7. D'Angelo, "Women Partners in the New Testament," 78.

called out by name as being loved by him. The text leads us to believe that the sisters have known Jesus for a while and a close friendship has developed over time. Mary and Martha presumably also are well aware of Jesus' ability to heal and, not surprisingly, expect his help with their brother's illness. They do not request his assistance explicitly, however, and the implication is that they assume Jesus naturally will come to their aid. Their closeness with him is evidenced first by the fact that they do not name their brother beyond "he whom you love." Second, their intimacy with Jesus is further indicated by the suggestion that they know how to get a message to him. This is significant because, in the previous chapter, Jesus escapes those trying to arrest him and hides himself across the Jordan (10:39–40), yet Mary and Martha know exactly how and where to find him.[8]

Mary's surroundings, then, are not unlike the secure environment in which a developing subject initially dwells. Her situation is evocative of Kristeva's concept of the semiotic *chora*, which she sees as a generative space, the birthplace of human subjectivity, the origin of all becoming. In fact, Kristeva draws the concept from Plato, whose Timaeus uses the term in the sense of a receptacle, a space in which the universe resides: "a fixed site for all things that come to be."[9] It is Plato's Timaeus who compares the *chora* to a nourishing and maternal presence, "a receptacle of being" that holds something and allows it to flourish.[10] In Kristeva's view, the developing child, prior to its emergence as a separate and definable subject, exists in a space much like this, a holding space shared with the mother. I propose that, in Mary's journey of developing selfhood, Jesus serves the function of the semiotic *chora*, acting as a holding space in which she will eventually flourish and her subjectivity will be birthed.

Kristeva's theory proposes that, within this realm of plenitude, the child experiences oneness with the maternal body, but is not able to distinguish itself as a discrete entity. Enjoying a sense of safety and protection with the mother, the child's functions and the child's connections with outside objects and family members are governed by this holding space.[11] In this world, the child is wholly dependent on the mother for responding to her needs. Mary's sending for Jesus in a time of crisis indicates a

---

8. Kitzberger, "Mary of Bethany," 573.
9. Plato, *Timaeus*, 41.
10. McAfee, *Julia Kristeva*, 19–20.
11. Kristeva, *Revolution in Poetic Language*, 25–35; McAfee, *Julia Kristeva*, 18–19, 35, 45.

reliance that is analogous to the child's dependence on the mother; it also reveals a presumption that he will provide safety and protection and will intervene on her behalf in difficult situations. Like the undeveloped subject who exists in undifferentiated oneness with the maternal body, Mary has not yet developed as an independent subject; at the same time, however, the *chora*-like environment will be the birthplace of her emerging subjectivity. In this way, the *chora* is both the space in which Mary is not yet a full and independent subject *and* the holding space for her eventual becoming; it is "the place where the subject is both generated and negated."[12]

Although Kristeva stresses that the semiotic *chora* is not a place or a space, she does conceptualize it spatially, as the "in-between" resulting from the relatedness of the developing child and its mother. This is where we first meet Mary, living in this "in-between," somewhere along the continuum in the development of her relationship with Jesus. She is a follower of Jesus, a disciple who is loved by him, so we know that she believes what he says to be true and trusts that he has the power to heal and perform miracles. Initially, Mary depends on Jesus and sees him as a teacher, friend, and miracle-worker, but as she emerges as a newly-constituted subject, she will understand him as much more.

Mary Before Receiving "the Word"

Just as the *chora* is not a place or a space, Kristeva argues that it is not a stage or phase either, yet she conceives of it temporally, as the time before symbolic language. For Kristeva, the development of subjectivity is inextricably linked with the development of language; she insists, in fact, that the study of language cannot be separated from the study of the "speaking being," the individual who is speaking, writing, or trying to express something—and whose living energy, drives, and wants imbue language with meaning. Speaking beings, or *parlêtres*, become who they are through the use of language, expressing themselves through what Kristeva calls the "signifying process"—the specific ways in which drives, desires, and needs are expressed through language.[13]

12. Kristeva, *Revolution in Poetic Language*, 28.

13. It is impossible to tease apart the various strands of Kristeva's thought, especially the overlap among the fields of philosophy, psychoanalytic theory, structural linguistics, and language/literary theory. Unlike other thinkers who see these as entirely separate fields of inquiry, "Kristeva shows that the speaking being is a 'strange fold' between them

The semiotic *chora*, then, is not only the foundation of subjectivity but also of language development, although it precedes the onset of language. Kristeva chooses the term *semiotic* because, in this space, meaning is produced—even though semiotic expression bears no resemblance to the symbolic language the child will later learn. The semiotic *chora* precedes Lacan's mirror stage and foreshadows the symbolic realm of language through its own form of language: rhythm and intonation, gesture and movement.[14] Yet, in this pre-verbal, pre-symbolic realm, there exists what Kristeva terms *motility*, the child's capability for spontaneous movement or responsiveness. Mary exhibits a similar reflexive responsiveness in the early part of her story. Initially, she does not speak, but it is possible to infer from the description of her actions that she responds spontaneously to others in her world, to events and experiences, and even to Jesus. Her movements, however, are limited and predictable—mimicking the developing child's early language of gesture and movement. Mary has not yet learned to express herself as a speaking being, but as she becomes an independent subject, she will learn a new way of communicating. She also has not yet understood Jesus as "the Word," but as she journeys toward subjectivity, she will receive him as the personified expression of God's presence in the world, the one who bestows the power to become a child of God.[15]

all—a place where . . . no border stands untouched by the forces on either side of it." McAfee, *Julia Kristeva*, 1, 13–15, 29.

14. Kristeva conceives of the semiotic *chora* as a place of becoming, and she considers the semiotic expressions of this realm to be as important as symbolic language; in fact, for her, this first form of language underlies the language of poetry and artistic creativity and is an essential dimension of all meaningful communication. The dynamic interplay of the semiotic and symbolic dimensions of language is explored later in this chapter.

15. A full exploration of the concept of Jesus as "the Word" is beyond the scope of this study, but it is helpful to review highlights of this theme. Brown explores Hellenistic origins for the Logos concept (Heraclitus, the Stoics, Philo, Hermetic literature, Mandean liturgies, and Gnosticism), finding in them meanings such as the "eternal principle of order in the universe," "the expression of the mind of God," "the intermediary between God and his creatures," or "a second God . . . the instrument of God in creation." In addition, he reviews possible Semitic origins (prophetic books of the Hebrew Bible, Deuteronomy, Psalms, and Wisdom of Solomon), and here he finds notions of the Logos as judge, life-giver, healer, creator, personified Wisdom, "the Law," a surrogate for God, or "the word . . . coming forth from the divine silence." Brown, *John I–XII*, 23–35 519–24. While there is no scholarly agreement as to the precise meaning of the Logos concept, for the purposes of this study, the focus is on "the Word" as divine revelation, God's presence on earth, coming into the world to empower believers to become God's children ("But to all who received him, who believed in his name, he gave power to become children of God"; 1:12). The opening words of John's Prologue ("in the beginning"), although they

The Not-Yet-Subject

Mary's Identity and Reliance on Jesus

Just as Mary's expressive ability is not yet fully developed, her self-understanding is incomplete, unformed; her identity is shaped by various images and identifications she encounters in the surrounding world. First and foremost, she and her sister appear to be firmly embedded in the Jewish community. The text announces that "many of the Jews had come out to Martha and Mary to console them about their brother" (11:19), but the wording in later verses places Mary in the center of this relationship with the Judeans: not only had they "come to her" (11:19), but also they "were with her in the house," "consoling her," "followed her" (11:31), "came with her" (11:33), and "had come with Mary" (11:45).[16] The suggestion here is that the Judeans are there to help and comfort Mary rather than her sister. Several scholars have noted the absence of hostile Jews in the John stories featuring women, but Mary's being with them in the mourning scene suggests not only an amicable relationship, but an intimacy and acceptance between the Judeans and Mary that we do not see in their interactions with other characters.[17] Here, Mary plays a role similar to that of the Samaritan woman in ch. 4—as an agent of reconciliation or liaison between various religious or ethnic groups.

In addition to (and in spite of) her close relationship with the Judeans, Mary also is identified as a disciple and follower of Jesus. When her sister returns home and announces to Mary that Jesus is calling for her (11:28), Martha speaks of him as "the teacher" (Ὁ διδάσκαλος), affirming that Mary and Martha are considered disciples of Jesus. As Dorothy Lee notes, Mary, Martha, and Lazarus, because of their intimate link to Jesus, are clearly indicated as disciples more than any other characters in the story.[18] Mary especially is one of the marginalized characters positioned as surpassing male disciples in terms of discipleship. When Jesus uses the metaphor of sleep in speaking to the disciples about Lazarus' death, for example, they

---

hearken back to a time before creation, suggest "that there is going to be a creation, a beginning" in our time. Ibid., 24. Becoming a child of God, then, is the birth from above that God effects through Jesus—and this is the new beginning hinted at in the opening verses of John.

16. Yamaguchi, *Mary and Martha*, 122.
17. Kitzberger, "Mary of Bethany," 578.
18. Lee, *Symbolic Narratives*, 199.

misunderstand him by interpreting his words literally. In addition, they display a lack of courage when they ask Jesus, "Rabbi, the Jews were just now trying to stone you, and are you going there again?" (11:8).[19] The negative depiction of the disciples in this chapter serves to underscore Mary's identity as a faithful disciple.

As she dwells in the *chora*-like environment of her relationship with Jesus—and supported by her connection with her family, the Judeans, and the community of Jesus' followers—Mary has not yet developed the boundaries of individual identity. Firmly established in these circles, her identity is defined by those around her, and she does not yet know what it means to be a child of God, one who is born from above. Kristeva reminds us that, at the same time the not-yet-subject longs to remain in the *chora*, the safe environment of the maternal body, she also must give it up if she is to become herself: "In order to become a subject, the child must renounce its identification with its mother; it must draw a line between itself and her."[20] As the not-yet-subject, Mary is unaware that her relationship with Jesus must change in order for her to become an independent self. Initially, she is secure in the connection, relying on Jesus' love and trusting that he will respond to her plea for help. Because Mary is aware that Jesus has healed others (the royal official's son, 4:46–54; the sick man by the pool, 5:2–15; the man born blind, 9:1–41), she has reason to believe that he will arrive in time to heal her brother. Yet, while her relationship with Jesus is positive, in order to move toward full personhood, she must give up her reliance on him and her need for him to mediate on her behalf.[21]

In addition, when her story begins, and even after her brother falls ill, Mary has not yet sensed real loss. Her brother has not yet died, nor has she experienced the absence of Jesus' support and responsiveness. This is similar to the developing child who, because she senses herself in oneness with the mother, does not experience herself as separate—or anything else

---

19. Stibbe, "Tomb with a View," 46.

20. McAfee, *Julia Kristeva*, 48.

21. The concept of Jesus as maternal figure is not entirely original. Dorothy Lee is one John scholar who alludes to Jesus' maternal role, highlighting several elements in the text as evidence: 1) his portrayal as the "one who nourishes the community of believers with his own 'flesh and blood'" (ch. 6); 2) the use of the word κοιλία (that can be translated as "womb") in the passage about "rivers of living water" flowing from Jesus (7:38); 3) statements made by Jesus that suggest a parental role ("I will not leave you as orphans"; 14:18); and 4) Jesus' giving of the beloved disciple and his mother to each other (19:26–27), suggesting his own role as "mother" to the disciples. Lee, *Flesh and Glory*, 148–55.

THE WORLD AS ILLUSION 51

for that matter; as a result, the child does not feel "absence." And because language has not yet emerged, the child does not distinguish between the real and the symbolic—a symbol standing in place of something real that is absent.[22] When Mary finally is prompted to speak later in the story, it is precisely loss, something real that is absent, which moves her to do so.

What Drives Mary?

At this point, however, it is not unreasonable to assume that Mary's spontaneous responses to others around her are driven primarily by family and kinship norms, expectations of groups in which she is embedded, and societal regulations. At the same time, although we cannot know Mary's inner mind, her actions over the course of the story point to the possibility of an inner desire that propels her toward rebirth, toward the alternative reality she has heard Jesus describe. This is not unlike the powerful drives Kristeva claims are involved in the early stages of subjectivity, "energy charges" that move through the body and, over the course of a subject's development, arrange themselves in response to outside family and social regulations. Because language is not yet present in the developing child, the semiotic *chora* functions as a sort of bridge, mediating between the not-yet-subject's inner drives and the outer environment of objects and family members. Vigorous and unpredictable, the drives produce a variety of bodily sensations and move the developing subject in many directions at once.[23] As we will see, Mary's movements and activities are not unlike these powerful drives involved in the early stages of subjectivity that move a not-yet-subject in many directions; her actions in the story appear to move her back and forth in an oscillating pattern that is an essential part of the process of her developing subjectivity.

Jesus as Mediator and Interpreter of the Law

For Kristeva, the mother's body is "the ordering principle of the semiotic *chora*," functioning as the regulator of the energies of the child's body—mediating conflicts between the not-yet-subject's inner drives and the outer symbolic law that organizes social relations. In our story, we can interpret

---

22. Payne, *Reading Theory*, 169.
23. Kristeva, *Revolution in Poetic Language*, 25.

Jesus as the mediator and ordering principle for Mary, guiding her in experiences and exchange with the larger world. As a follower of Jesus, she has been privy to his teachings about the need to be born from above, born of God, and born of the Spirit (1:13; 3:3, 5, 6, 7, 8), as well as his message about eternal life (3:15, 16, 36; 4:14, 36; 5:24, 39; 6:27, 40, 47, 54, 68; 10:28; 12:25, 50; 17:2, 3). As she negotiates what may be an inner drive toward new birth, eternal life, and "the world above"—and pressures from the outer world of the traditional Jewish law and "the world below"—Jesus serves to mediate any conflicts between the two, specifically conflicts between the Jewish law and the new revelation he brings. While the traditional Jewish law and external regulations are what order Mary's life now, eventually she will learn the truth that comes from God through Jesus—"The law indeed was given through Moses; grace and truth came through Jesus Christ" (1:17)—and embrace the renewed "law" that he teaches.

Jesus urges believers to follow the law that "was given through Moses," (ὁ νόμος διὰ Μωυσέως ἐδόθη; 1:17, 45; 7:19, 23; 8:5), and the word itself (νόμος) is indicative of "a force or influence impelling to action"—suggesting that the law of the Judeans is an external force compelling believers to behave in a certain way. But there also is a strong suggestion that Jesus sets himself apart from the law (8:17; 10:34; 15:25; 18:31; 19:7). He reveals the existing law as an inadequate guideline for living, and he implements a new guideline for his community of followers, which he refers to as "a new commandment" (ἐντολὴν καινὴν; 13:34). This commandment is specifically a call to love: "I give you a new commandment, that you love one another. Just as I have loved you, you also should love one another" (13:34; 14:15, 21; 15:10, 12, 14, 17).

Jesus' "commandment" evokes Kristeva's idea of a pre-existing maternal law that exists in the semiotic *chora* long before the "Law of the Father."[24] While Freud and Lacan argue that it is the paternal function and law that propel the developing child into social organization, Kristeva contends that what moves an infant beyond the *chora* is something else entirely. Countering the Freud-Lacan idea that castration threats are what fuel the child's developing subjectivity, Kristeva contends that fear is not a strong enough motivation for leaving the safety and comfort of the maternal body. She points to the process of abjection—whereby the child separates from the mother—as the catalyst for the child's movement out of the safety of the

---

24. Kristeva, *Revolution in Poetic Language*, 25–28; Oliver, *Reading Kristeva*, 3–4; Payne, *Reading Theory*, 169.

chora. The experience of abjection, because it occurs when the child still exists in an imaginary oneness with the mother, is vital to moving the child to the next stage in her developing subjectivity. Like the developing subject, Mary also is not motivated by "paternal law" in her journey to selfhood.[25] Jesus is, for Mary and his other followers, a mediator and re-interpreter of the existing law of social exchange: "If a man receives circumcision on the Sabbath in order that the law of Moses may not be broken, are you angry with me because I healed a man's whole body on the Sabbath?" (7:23). In Mary's story so far, the law of the Judeans, a law based largely on fear, has not been enough to propel her to a new life or a new self. What propels her toward a new subjectivity is the opposite of the law, in fact. It is her own internal drive, a desire for new birth, *and* Jesus' presence as the revelation of God that effects her rebirth into new life.

Challenging the father-centered theories of Freud and Lacan, Kristeva highlights the role of the mother in the movement toward selfhood; she claims that the mothering figure plays a momentous role in creating the environment for developing subjectivity. Just as Jesus serves as the semiotic *chora* and maternal figure for Mary, his role in her journey toward subjectivity is to create an environment for her birth from above, to facilitate her entry into an alternative world, and to foster a relationship of abiding oneness with God.

---

25. Cultural anthropology tells us that first-century Palestine was a society based on collectivism rather than individualism; persons living in this culture were embedded in groups, and their individual concerns were oriented toward the concerns of the group. Important in this culture was the need to maintain honor and status for the group by living out the expectations of other persons, and individuals' self-image derived from what others both inside and outside the group thought of them. Malina, *New Testament World*, 61–62. Our present-day pre-occupation with the individual self did not exist for first-century Palestinians: "the Western conception of the person as a bounded, unique, more or less integrated motivational and cognitive universe, a dynamic center of awareness, emotion, judgment, and action organized into a distinctive whole and set contrastively both against other such wholes and against its social and natural background." Geertz, *Local Knowledge*, 59. Neither the Fourth Evangelist nor his audience would have concerned themselves with one individual person's development. This interpretation, however, is concerned precisely with this issue, particularly the way it can inform our understanding of new birth and the journey toward selfhood.

Abjection

Mary's Encounter with Death

Although Mary is not present for the conversation between Jesus and the disciples about Lazarus' illness, (11:7–16), the dialogue highlights his followers' naïve view of death. When Jesus uses the metaphor of sleep to refer to Lazarus' condition, he is referring to its temporary nature—one that will be overturned by his being raised up—but the disciples misunderstand. At worst, they interpret his statement literally, as if Lazarus has fallen asleep and is resting; at best, their confusion causes them to view death as an illusion, something akin to falling asleep. Jesus must clarify, and he does so with the blunt statement that "Lazarus is dead" (11:14). His statement breaks the disciples' view of death as unreal or an allusion, awakening them to the fact that "death is brutally real."[26] From this perspective, we can see that Jesus understands the terrible reality of human death and does not dismiss it as a lack of faith in his power to bring life.

This brutal reality of death has broken through in Mary's life as well. It is likely that the loss of her brother reverberates on several levels. First, the death of a sibling, especially in a family without parents, is a significant personal sorrow. Second, although the family appears relatively comfortable, the loss of a supporting male in the lives of two unmarried women is bound to produce financial uncertainty.[27] And finally, the implications of Jesus' absence at the time of Lazarus' death, when presumably he could have been present to help, adds another layer to Mary's loss.

It is likely that Mary is experiencing not only sorrow over these very real losses, but also the sense of abjection that death engenders. Kristeva argues that abjection not only is essential for the development of human subjectivity in early infancy, but also occurs throughout the course of a life. Much more than separation from the mother, abjection is something an individual experiences throughout life at moments of extreme crisis, suffering, horror, or taboo. It can occur with any crisis, a violent dynamic that shapes the human subject not just in early development but continuously throughout life: "pre-symbolic, abjection yet persists and returns in flashes, at places of strain or moments of crisis within the symbolic system."[28]

---

26. Schneiders, "Death in the Community," 49.
27. Malina and Rohrbaugh, *John*, 195.
28. Becker-Leckrone, *Julia Kristeva*, 31–32.

THE WORLD AS ILLUSION 55

Mary's experience with death, and her abjection of the idea of death, is likely to be amplified by an encounter with her brother's dead body. One of the most disorienting moments of abjection occurs, Kristeva tells us, upon the shock of seeing a corpse—an encounter like no other. The utmost of abjection, seeing a cadaver is an experience that threatens the boundaries of life and order and pushes us to the border of our condition as living beings. Kristeva reminds us that a dead body is not a *signifier* of death, as a flat encephalograph might be; instead, it is "death infecting life," showing us what we all ultimately must become. In encountering a cadaver, an individual is faced with the prospect of her own annihilation, and the border is permeated that once protected her as a living human from death:

> That elsewhere that I imagine beyond the present . . . it is now here, jetted, abjected into "my world" . . . In that compelling, raw, insolent thing in the morgue's full sunlight . . . I behold the breaking down of a world that has erased its borders . . .[29]

Although the text does not tell us who prepares Lazarus' body for burial, it is almost certainly Mary and Martha who do so. Because they are depicted as being in close communion with the Jewish community, we can assume also that they keep to the traditional mourning practices of Judaism as detailed in the Hebrew Scriptures. In their world, impurity (*tum'ah*) is seen as being passed along by corpses; in handling their brother's body, then, the sisters would be considered unclean or defiled. A human corpse, in fact, is the ultimate and most intense source of defilement. For the first seven days after a death, relatives of the deceased undergo an intensive time of mourning, refraining from certain everyday activities such as cutting one's hair, working, washing one's clothes, etc. An individual who has encountered a corpse and become defiled needs purification or cleaning, and the seven-day period ensures this.[30] These practices, Kristeva would argue, are a living illustration of her notion of abjection and the need to create boundaries between the subject and that which is "abjected."

Once she is defiled by the handling of a corpse, Mary also would be subject to certain restrictions such as not being able to participate in Temple worship or enter the sanctuary. Since biblical legislation requires that which is unclean to be kept separate from anything holy, someone

---

29. Kristeva, *Powers of Horror*, 3–4.
30. Feldman, *Biblical and Post-Biblical Defilement*, 15, 33–34.

unclean is prohibited from any communion with the Divine.[31] With these restrictions likely guiding her actions, Mary is essentially separated from communal religious and spiritual life; when we see her in mourning with the Judeans, for example, she is in the privacy of her home rather than in the Temple (11:20).

At this point in the story, having felt acutely the termination of life, Mary experiences the absence of life and the absence of holiness. As the absence of life, death also is the absence of God, so a mourner such as Mary is desacralized: "death and holiness are not compatible."[32] As she experiences the reality and tangible nature of death, her relationship with the Divine is temporarily severed and she is estranged from God. In witnessing the exact opposite of a living human being—death—Mary is now an "incomplete person," and it is as if she herself were dead. Emanuel Feldman describes the experience of the mourner:

> He has been touched by the anti-life aspects of *tum'ah* and he himself therefore becomes less lifelike, less complete as a human being. His brush with death and *tum'ah* causes him, at least for the moment, to lose his identity as a person and as a human. For just as *tum'ah* separates man from God, it also separates man from the fraternity and community of other men, and separates man from his essential self, from his essence as a person. In the face of the Ultimate Category of *tum'ah*, the human being ceases to exist as a person.[33]

In entering into close contact with death and a state of uncleanness, then, Mary is temporarily separated from others in her community, from God, and from herself as a person. Her experience of abjection is "a gravitational field that summons the subject from its proper place to a no-man's land where the subject . . . almost ceases to be."[34]

In his study of death and mourning in the biblical world, Feldman also suggests a connection between uncleanness and a sense of lack: "Since the otherwise common Semitic word for 'be thirsty' does not seem to appear anywhere in Aramaic it seems to be more than likely, from the etymological point of view, that the word 'to be unclean' meant originally 'to be lacking, to be wanting'. . . the Latin word *satis*, 'thirst' and the corresponding verb

---

31. Ibid., 15.
32. Ibid., 35.
33. Ibid., 93.
34. Becker-Leckrone, *Julia Kristeva*, 33.

also have the double meaning of 'thirst' and 'want' or 'lack.'"[35] Mary, in her liminal state of mourning, having experienced the reality of death, can be understood as "thirsting" or "yearning" for whatever it is that will bring her new life. She is in an in-between place, suspended between the life and world she thought she knew—and believed she could rely on—and a new reality that she is not yet able to imagine.

The Narcissistic Structure

Jesus Delays His Response

When Jesus hears the message from Mary and Martha that their brother is sick, his response is spoken not just for the disciples within hearing range or for the one bringing the message, but for all. Some commentators go so far as to propose that the messenger returns to the sisters with Jesus' words, which are "designed to suggest hope to the sisters when all hope was over."[36] What we do know is that, instead of rushing directly to aid of the friends he loves, Jesus remains two days longer before going to Bethany (11:6). Mary and Martha do not know what Jesus knows—that Lazarus already was dead when he received the news. When Jesus does draw near to the village, in fact, he discovers that Lazarus has already been dead four days (11:17), yet he himself only has delayed his arrival for two days. As readers, we know then that Jesus' absence does not cause Lazarus' death.[37] Mary, however, must question how Jesus could allow her brother to die when, as the Jews later wonder, "Could not he who opened the eyes of the blind man have kept this man from dying?" (11:37). Jesus' disciples have heard him teaching about a divine and eternal life—"Very truly, I tell you, whoever keeps my word will never see death" (8:51) and "I came that they may have life, and have it abundantly" (10:10)—and, for them, the presence of death is confounding and can only be the result of Jesus' absence.

Jesus explains the reason for his delay as the opportunity for his disciples to believe what he has been teaching them: "For your sake I am glad I was not there, so that you may believe" (11:15). Reading this verse in tandem with Jesus' earlier comment—that Lazarus' "illness" occurred so

---

35. Feldman, *Biblical and Post-Biblical Defilement*, 74.

36. Westcott, *John*, 164–65.

37. Moloney, "Can Everyone Be Wrong?," 515–19; Moloney, "Faith of Martha and Mary," 480–89.

that he (Jesus) "may be glorified through it" (11:4)—indicates that Jesus wants the disciples to see the miracle he is about to perform, so that they may come to believe (ἵνα πιστεύσητε; 11:15) that he is the revelation of God. The challenge facing Jesus' disciples, including Mary, then, is how to understand death in the context of eternal life and how it relates to Jesus' presence and absence.[38] It is clear to the reader that the ultimate purpose of the coming events is not for the sake of Lazarus but for something more— to bring others to authentic faith in Jesus.[39]

Mark W. G. Stibbe points to another dimension of Jesus' characterization in John's gospel that sheds light on this passage: his mysterious elusiveness. According to Stibbe, Jesus' elusiveness is evident in actions such as his withdrawal in the face of danger, his escapes, his secret movements, or uncertainty about his physical location. We also note an elusive dimension of Jesus' discourse—his use of metaphorical language, cryptic statements, and discontinuous dialogue.[40] In this chapter of John, we see several examples of elusiveness in Jesus' actions: his delay in responding to Mary and Martha's message that Lazarus is ill and, when he finally does arrive in Bethany, his decision to remain outside the village. Similarly, Jesus' language is evasive, as evident in his cryptic statement that Lazarus' "illness does not lead to death" (11:4), his question to the disciples, "are there not twelve hours of daylight?" (11:9), and his use of the metaphor of sleep when warning the disciples that Lazarus has died (11:11). For Stibbe, the purpose of Jesus' elusiveness is to point to a mysterious God who cannot be apprehended and, at the same time, to continually direct attention to another, radically transcendent realm.[41]

Stibbe's study highlights Jesus' focus on the transcendent realm of the world above, the realm of new birth. When read through this lens, these verses reflect the theme of eternal life and the paradoxical notion that through death comes new life. Jesus' delay in responding, then, can be understood as his desire to help believers wrestle with the reality of death and his (Jesus') ultimate role in bringing new life—or rebirth. It is, in part, through Jesus' actions in this chapter that Mary's transformation is accomplished.

---

38. Schneiders, "Death in the Community," 48.
39. Moloney, *Signs and Shadows*, 159.
40 Stibbe, "Elusive Christ," 20–28; Stibbe, "Tomb with a View," 44.
41 Stibbe, "Elusive Christ," 28.

An Act of Love

Jesus' failure to respond is not a failure of love for Mary, her sister, or Lazarus. Both Jesus' delay and his eventual actions are the result of his divine love and divine knowledge; he goes to the family not when asked, but when he knows his arrival will be most helpful.[42] Schneiders argues, in fact, that the text says exactly this by linking two seemingly contradictory statements: "Accordingly, though Jesus loved Martha and her sister and Lazarus, after having heard that Lazarus was ill, he stayed two days longer in the place where he was" (11:5–6). Jesus appears to be absent, yet he knows what is happening to Lazarus (11:14) and what it means (11:4–5). Schneiders points out that "not only is absence compatible with love, it can even be the expression of love."[43]

If Jesus' decision not to respond to the sisters immediately is an act of love, it is analogous to the gradual separation of the developing child from the mother in the early stages of life. Kristeva points to a moment in the developing child's struggle, prior to the emergence of the self, in which she feels acutely the loss of the mother. This emerges as a "parting sadness" that the child feels as she resigns herself to the inevitable and accepts the loss of the mother's body. The loss that the child experiences in the separation of the mother's body is an emptiness, a deprivation similar to Freud's death drive. Because the child is not able to articulate such loss, she pushes away the very thing that is missing, carving out a space for herself—and for symbolic language to emerge—and triggering the mechanism of abjection. In this way, loss underlies all abjection—and abjection functions as the child's protection against the despair of this loss.[44]

Mary's Metaphorical Death

The fact that the Jews assume Mary is going to the tomb to weep there reflects the depth of grief and emotionality she experiences that her sister does not. The verb used to describe Mary's implied mourning (κλαίω; "to mourn," "to weep," "to bewail," or "to lament";[45] 11:31) is strongly suggestive

---

42. Westcott, *John*, 165.
43. Schneiders, "Death in the Community," 51.
44. Kristeva, *Black Sun*, 9–10; Kristeva, *Powers of Horror*, 9–10; Beardsworth, *Julia Kristeva*, 98–104.
45. Danker, *Greek-English Lexicon*, 545.

of a "continuous, almost passionate, expression of sorrow."[46] In addition, her near-silence as she grieves for her brother is a behavior typically associated with mourning and lamenting. In her world, silence during the period after a close relative's death would be considered an essential element of mourning and an appropriate expression of grief. Silence signifies the desacralization of the mourner and his diminished condition as a person: as the mourner refrains from everyday talk, he "expresses in silence the new status which is his as the result of his contact with death and *tum'ah*."[47]

Thomas' comment to his fellow-disciples, "Let us also go, that we may die with him" (11:16), can inform this reading of Mary's state of mourning. Thomas' remark suggests that he finally understands Lazarus' passing as something other than mere death. Barrett offers an intriguing insight about this comment, that it is a statement of an unconscious truth, that "the journey into Judaea is for the purpose of death, and later dying with Christ will become the characteristic mark of Christian discipleship."[48] The implication is that believers must die a metaphorical death in order to be healed, whole, and saved; they must not only die to "the world below," but also they must leave their former lives and selves behind. Mary is in the process of this kind of metaphorical death as she experiences separation from her brother, from her community, and from Jesus. Her immersion in mourning can be likened to what the child in the process of developing subjectivity experiences—a stage in which the child begins to be aware that her surroundings are different from herself, that the union she has felt with her mother is not real. As she begins to sense that things are not as they appear, she begins to renounce her identity with her mother. Mary's security in her relationship with Jesus—her presumption that, out of love for her family, he would come to their aid and heal her brother—has now been ruptured. She has discovered that the union she thought she had with Jesus is not what she imagined it to be.

Mary Turns Away from Jesus

Mary's grief is compounded by loss; her actions suggest that she experiences pain not only over the death of her brother, but also over Jesus' absence and what it appears to mean. Although the text does not state this, we can

---

46. Westcott, *John*, 170.
47. Feldman, *Biblical and Post-Biblical Defilement*, 97–99.
48. Barrett, *John*, 327–28.

THE WORLD AS ILLUSION   61

assume that Mary knows as well as Martha that Jesus is near the village, yet Mary chooses to stay at home with the Jews, who are consoling her. When it is clear that Jesus has arrived and is outside of Bethany, only Martha goes out to meet him. Mary is described as being in the house, sitting still and stationary (ἐκαθέζετο;[49] 11:20), which is considered the traditional posture for mourners.[50] While some commentators interpret Mary's staying at home as the expected practice of mourning, when considered in conjunction with her other actions, it differentiates her from her sister and leaves readers with the impression that Mary is ambivalent about Jesus.[51] Her initial reluctance to meet Jesus is an indication of her grief and disappointment, but it also suggests something else about her emotional state—the fact that something has changed dramatically, that she has lost hope, that she has lost her naiveté about what it means to be loved by Jesus. Not only does Mary experience abjection of her brother's corpse and of death itself, then, but the story suggests that she, in her grief and disappointment, also turns away from Jesus temporarily. Like the developing child who must abject the mother during the earliest stages of subjectivity, Mary must relinquish her dependence on Jesus in order to become herself.[52]

Mary's turning away from Jesus bears signs of a developing subject's separation from its mother, what Kristeva suggests is not only the first experience of abjection but also the most powerful.[53] The phenomenon of

49. Danker, *Greek-English Lexicon*, 490.

50. Moloney, *Signs and Shadows*, 161.

51. Moloney, "Can Everyone Be Wrong?," 517 n. 42.

52. Mary's abjection of Jesus can be understood in the context of the ultimate abjection he faces at the hands of his opponents. Her temporary rejection of Jesus may be a lower octave of that, as she begins to see him as wholly Other and wonders, *Who is this man I thought I knew?*

53. Kristeva's concept of the semiotic *chora* has come under criticism by feminist scholars, some of whom characterize it as a regression to patriarchal understandings of femininity that limit a woman's role to motherhood and serving as a "maternal uterus." Butler, "Body Politics of Julia Kristeva," 104–18. Kristeva's theory of abjection also has come under criticism for conceiving the movement from "One" (child and mother) to the "Other" (speaking subject) as a violent break that fosters gendered oppositions such as spirit and matter. Kristeva's concept of what constitutes both the human subject and the onset of language is considered by some critics to be a "double denial, namely the denial of woman as the m/other of Logos and the denial of the other as feminine." Margaroni, "Lost Foundation," 81–82. Kristeva makes it clear that the maternal function is served not only by a mother or a woman; the function of meeting the needs of the child can be fulfilled by either gender. And, while she is careful not to reduce motherhood to an inevitable function of the female, at the same time, she acknowledges that, in patriarchal

abjecting the mother is significant in that it marks three pivotal events: the child's growing discovery of the external world; the onset of the child's entry into the symbolic realm; and the beginning development of the child's subjectivity—"as the 'I' discovers what is 'not-I,' what is other . . ."[54] As long as the infant remained in imaginary oneness with the maternal body in the *chora*, there were no borders. Through the process of abjection, however, the child is able to differentiate its own body from the abject maternal body, and she begins to develop borders between "I" and others. This is the beginning of the child's identity as a self separate from others.[55]

Kristeva calls abjection of the mother a "narcissistic crisis," a crisis of understanding that the union with the mother was not real. Even as the child needs to surrender the union with its mother, she still longs for what she has lost. And even as the mother is lost to the child, she remains "as an ambivalent love-hatred for an object that is not lost but preserved within."[56] Kristeva makes clear that is abject is not entirely gone: "The abject continues to haunt the subject's consciousness, remaining on the periphery of awareness . . . the subject finds the abject both repellant and seductive and thus his or her borders of self are, paradoxically, continuously threatened and maintained."[57]

At its most basic, abjection involves a crisis in the developing subject's perception of the borders that separate self from Other, a struggle with the permeability of the borders of inside and outside. It is a crisis involving *place*: "ambiguous borderlines and unmapped frontiers, of strays and exiles and outcasts."[58] We can see Mary as the not-yet-subject in exile, separated from her community, and feeling dispossessed by Jesus, someone she has loved and has loved her. She cannot go back, and she cannot go forward; she remains in a "nowhere" space, not belonging to any one place.

The emerging subject must learn to deal with the impact of the loss and dislocation, yet does not have language to negotiate or express it. While the child's abjection of the maternal body in infancy is what allows the

---

cultures that see women only in the maternal/reproductive function, a problem arises in that females become associated with abjection. If becoming a subject requires abjection of the feminine, then, "within patriarchy, women, maternity, and femininity are all abjected along with the maternal function." Oliver, "Kristeva and Feminism," lines 42–43.

54. Ward, *Christ and Culture*, 209.
55. Kristeva, *Powers of Horror*, 4; McAfee, *Julia Kristeva*, 46.
56. Beardsworth, *Julia Kristeva*, 99.
57. McAfee, *Julia Kristeva*, 49–50.
58. Becker-Leckrone, *Julia Kristeva*, 32; Beardsworth, *Julia Kristeva*, 81–83.

development of boundaries and identity in the first place, when abjection occurs at other times in life, it threatens those same borders. The abject—whether filth, or food, or death—is associated with what is Other *to* us, yet it began with what is Other *within* us (the maternal body). This means that the abject remains, always with us on the border of consciousness, never fully eliminated and always blurring and threatening the boundaries between Self and Other. The abject represents the ambiguous, the "in-between." It remains on the border threatening the unity and identity of the subject and calling into question the established order of society.[59] According to Kristeva, the abject is "a terror that dissembles, a hatred that smiles, a passion that uses the body for barter instead of inflaming it, a debtor who sells you up, a friend who stabs you . . ."[60] Although Jesus' failure to respond to Mary and Martha may be, in fact, an expression of love, Mary experiences it as something shocking and unexpected that is wholly foreign to her. Through his actions in this scene, Jesus is the "in-between" who not only threatens Mary's identity, but also causes her to have an experience "in which the borders of Self and Other radically break down."[61] Although it is necessary for Mary to turn away from Jesus in order to develop an authentic and stable self, while she is in the process, her identity remains vulnerable and unstable.[62] Yet her disavowal of Jesus is temporary and incomplete because, as Kristeva reminds us, the abject is always with us on the border of consciousness.

Kristeva also clarifies that abjection of the Other is an abjection of one's self—precisely because that which is abjected appears to be part of the subject who, in desiring the abject, is "homologous" to it. Abjection is both disruptive and constitutive of the self, then:[63] "I expel *myself*, I spit *myself* out, I abject *myself* within the same motion through which 'I' claim to establish *myself*."[64] Abjection and desire, in Kristeva's view, are inextricably related: it is in the act of abjection that one re-encounters the original loss

---

59. Kristeva, *Powers of Horror*, 4; McAfee, *Julia Kristeva*, 49; Oliver, *Reading Kristeva*, 56.
60. Kristeva, *Powers of Horror*, 4.
61. Becker-Leckrone, *Julia Kristeva*, 151, 32–34.
62. Grosz, "The Body of Signification," 86.
63. Keltner, *Kristeva: Thresholds*, 45.
64. Kristeva, *Powers of Horror*, 3.

of the maternal body, "the inaugural loss," the "want on which any being, meaning, language, or desire is founded."[65]

We can imagine that Mary, in turning away from Jesus, may return to that inaugural loss experienced in infancy. In abjecting him, she also may sense *herself* as abject. This calls to mind an important distinction Freud makes in his seminal essay, "Mourning and Melancholia." In his view, profound mourning is a natural reaction to the loss of a loved one and involves a loss of interest in the outside world, an inability to develop new love, and a cessation of all usual activity. In some cases, however, the person in mourning also experiences melancholia—a condition that bears all the hallmarks of mourning but which also is characterized by a disturbance in self-regard, a loss of self-love. The melancholy mourner, Freud argues, in addition to consciously mourning the loss of a loved one, also is unconsciously mourning the loss of a loved "object" that cannot be replaced. Freud describes it in this way:

> An object-choice, an attachment of the libido to a particular person, had at one time existed; then, owing to a real slight or disappointment coming from this loved person, the object-relationship was shattered.[66]

As the mourner experiences the shattering of this object relationship, her feelings about the slight or disappointment are shifted from the loved one to the mourner herself.[67] It is quite likely that Mary, out of sorrow, disappointment, and a sense of being abandoned by Jesus, directs toward *herself* feelings she does not express to him directly.

The Purpose of Mary's Sorrow

Jesus' actions suggest that his intent is for Mary and Martha—and the disciples—to experience the full force of their grief and loss before he arrives to help. Craig Keener's claim that "John's teaching is that suffering can provide the opportunity for divine intervention . . ."[68] touches on only one dimension of this experience. In our story, suffering also awakens the disciples—especially Mary—to the limitations of human existence, forcing

---

65. Ibid., 5.
66. Freud, "Mourning and Melancholia," 248–49.
67. Ibid., 246–49.
68. Keener, *John*, 2:839.

them to move beyond the prosaic concerns of their daily lives and opening to a brand new kind of life. Yet, Mary is the only one to do this.

Commentators who interpret Mary's actions in ch. 11 as weak or passive tend to focus on what they see as her mistaken understanding of what Lazarus' death means, her failure to recognize the significance of Jesus' presence, and her inability to "transcend the human pain and sorrow generated by the death of a loved one."[69] My interpretation proposes that it is precisely Mary's inability to immediately step beyond human pain and sorrow that leads to her rebirth. Kristeva's theory of abjection reminds us that "subjectivity originates in crisis and, significantly, remains in crisis."[70]

The Thetic Break

Mary is Called by Jesus

As the story progresses, Mary's significance as a friend of Jesus and as a disciple is made clear: she is called personally by Jesus (Ὁ διδάσκαλος πάρεστιν καὶ φωνεῖ σε; 11:28). The use of the verb φωνέω ("to speak loud or clearly," "to cry out to," "to call for," "to call to one's self," or "to call out of"), as opposed to the more common καλέω ("to call by name" or "to summon"),[71] is significant. Here, the verb is the same as the one used later in the narrative by Jesus when he calls Lazarus to life (11:43); it is, in fact, used on several occasions to call individuals to true faith (3.8, 29; 5:25, 28; 10:3, 4, 16, 27), and it is always "a call to the fullness of life with him."[72] Just as the sheep listen to, hear, and know Jesus' voice, so does Mary. The word φωνέω indicates an animating, awakening, or calling forth rather than a summons or command. Jesus' "calling" Mary in this manner suggests that he is calling her to presence and new life, and some part of her senses she is being "called forth by the word of Jesus."[73]

Mary also is moving into a larger world. Stibbe, the scholar who describes Jesus' elusiveness, highlights another narrative technique that can inform our understanding of actions in this scene—"external focalization,"

---

69. Moloney, "Can Everyone Be Wrong?," 518.
70. Becker-Leckrone, *Julia Kristeva*, 30.
71. Danker, *Greek-English Lexicon*, 1071, 502–3.
72. Moloney, "Faith of Martha and Mary," 480; Moloney, "Can Everyone Be Wrong?," 516.
73. Moloney, "Faith of Martha and Mary," 481.

which helps readers focus on a character's movement. When the narrative begins at the start of this chapter, Jesus is outside of Judea, and there is a movement to return to Judea, "Let us go to Judea again" (11:7; also in 11:8, 16). Next, Jesus moves to just outside of Bethany, "Now Jesus had not yet come to the village" (11:30; also in 11:20). Finally, in the next segment of the text, we see Jesus move to outside the tomb of Lazarus, "Then Jesus, again greatly disturbed, came to the tomb" (11:38). In this example of external focalization, John gives a sense of Jesus' movement from one place to another, moving eventually to the focus of the story, Lazarus' tomb.[74] Stibbe's analysis also can be applied to Mary's movement from one place to another: she first stays at home (11:20), then ultimately, she leaves her home, the traditional domain of the woman, to go to the place outside the village where Jesus waits (11:29–30), and finally it appears that she too moves to the tomb (11:34). While the movement of Jesus is increasingly inward, Mary, in the initial stages of developing subjectivity, gradually moves outward from the protection and comfort of her home to a larger, new, and different world.

The presence of the Judeans with Mary also helps set the stage for her movement into a new territory and being caught in a liminal place between two worlds—the world above and the world below. While they assume that she is going to the tomb to weep (v. 31), she is, in fact, responding to the call of Jesus, a going forth that transcends their earth-bound concerns. This "clash of worlds: that which flows from the presence of Jesus . . . and that which flows from accepted religious, cultural, and historical custom"[75] introduces the idea that Mary is moving into new territory—toward rebirth and fuller subjectivity.

Mary Hopes in Jesus Again

Yet one verse sets Mary apart from the Judeans, indicating that she alone is making the journey toward rebirth; Martha tells Mary "secretly" (λάθρα; 11:28) that Jesus is calling for her. The verb used to describe Mary's hearing his call—to "hear" or "give ear to" (ἀκούω;[76] 11:29) is used consistently throughout John's gospel—along with to "come unto him" (ἔρχομαι πρὸς αὐτόν; 11:29)—as a way of stating the act of believing in Jesus. Here, the verb ἀκούω ("to hear," "to give ear," "to hearken") is reminiscent of earlier

74. Stibbe, "Tomb with a View," 42–43.
75. Moloney, "Faith of Mary and Martha," 482.
76. Danker, *Greek-English Lexicon*, 37.

descriptions of an individual responding positively to the word of Jesus (1:37, 40; 3:8, 29, 32; 4:42, 47; 5:24, 25, 28, 30; 6:45; 7:40, 51; and 8:47), suggesting that Mary, in spite of turning away from Jesus temporarily, has retained a sense of openness to hearing what he has to say.[77]

Mary's Awakening

The language of the text also supports the idea of Mary's movement toward a fuller life. In his earlier conversation with the disciples about Lazarus being "asleep," Jesus says to them, "I am going there to awaken him" (ἀλλὰ πορεύομαι ἵνα ἐξυπνίσω αὐτόν; 11:11). The verb is ἐξυπνίζω, which means "to wake up," "to arouse," or "to awaken out of sleep." The disciples misunderstand Jesus, of course, taking his words literally and responding, "Lord, if he has fallen asleep, he will be all right" (εἰ κεκοίμηται σωθήσεται; 11:12). The verb used by the disciples here, σώζω, can be translated in a variety of ways to indicate ether physical healing or spiritual salvation: "to save," "to make sound," "to preserve," "to heal," "to restore to health," "to make well," or "to save from death and judgment"[78]—and this same verb is used several times in John's gospel to indication salvation (3:17; 5:34; 10:9; 12:47).

Similarly, in the passage where Mary hears that Jesus is near Bethany, she responds immediately, "And when she heard it, she got up quickly and went to him" (ἐκείνη δὲ ὡς ἤκουσεν ἠγέρθη ταχὺ καὶ ἤρχετο πρὸς αὐτόν; 11:29). Here, the verb used to describe Mary's actions is ἐγείρω, which can be translated as "to awaken," "to arouse," "to rouse from sleep," or "to wake up from the sleep of death." It also can mean "to heal," "to raise to life," or "to cause to be born" and, in several instances in John, it is used to indicate being raised from the dead (2:22; 5:21; 12:1, 9, 17, 14). Further, when the Jews notice Mary "get up quickly and go out" (ταχέως ἀνέστη καὶ ἐξῆλθεν; 11:31), the verb is ἀνίστημι, also meaning "to raise up (as the dead)," "to raise up into existence," "to raise up by bringing back to life," or "to cause to be born"[79] (6:39, 40, 44, 54; 11:23, 24; 20:9).

The overlapping meanings of these verbs—referring to the raising of Lazarus, believers, or Jesus from the dead—suggests that Mary also is in need of being awakened to the fullness of life, restored to wholeness, or raised from the dead. In Kristevan terms, Mary rests still in the safety and

---

77. Moloney, "Faith of Mary and Martha," 481.
78. Danker, *Greek-English Lexicon*, 354, 982.
79. Ibid., 271, 83.

dependence of the semiotic *chora*, but she is in the process of moving toward a larger world and becoming an independent subject.

Mary's Receptivity

When she reaches Jesus, she falls at his feet (ἔπεσεν αὐτοῦ πρὸς τοὺς πόδας; 11:32), indicating a state of not only respectfulness but also receptivity. Mary says exactly the words her sister said earlier, "Lord, if you had been here, my brother would not have died" (11:32). Although Mary says the same words, her demeanor introduces a different tone to the conversation. Whereas Martha appears reproachful, almost resentful with Jesus, Mary's presence indicates a different set of emotions. She has waited to be called forth by Jesus rather than confronting him as Martha has done, and she speaks to Jesus from a prostrate position as opposed to the face-to-face conversation Martha has with him. Although initially disappointed in his lack of response, Mary appears to convey a sense of openness, respect, and receptivity—even in the midst of sorrow.

Mary Speaks

Mary's gestures, demeanor, and words illustrate one of Kristeva's key concepts—the fact that meaning can be present in the body and expressed without formal language—the way a child can signify meaning before knowing words or the elements of symbolic language through the use of rhythms and intonations, sounds and gestures. While in this stage, the child does not understand that these noises have meaning, but over time, begins to see that utterances can signify objects or needs or wants. This ability to point to something beyond the self leads to the child's growing awareness of the distinction between Self and Other. Kristeva dubs this the "thetic phase" and sees it as the jumping-off point for the development of language—"the threshold of language"—*and* the development of subjectivity. The thetic break occurs when the child becomes aware of herself as a separate subject and is able to point to something outside herself.[80] Kristeva further describes the thetic break as a kind of boundary between semiotic and symbolic language, unifying and structuring semiotic energy into symbolic forms that can be recognized as coherent meaning. The child

80. Kristeva, *Revolution in Poetic Language*, 43–46.

becomes ready to use language symbolically, but does not leave the semiotic realm behind. In Kristeva's view, however, the thetic is a phase rather than a solid boundary between the two realms; it is permeable in the sense that the subject may move in and out of this phase as her subjectivity develops.[81]

Kristeva contends that a child's entry into symbolic language is marked by a sense of absence: The child senses lack and a simultaneous desire for that which is absent. Prior to this, the mother-child symbiosis has allowed the child to experience need and fulfillment before desire emerges out of a sense of something absent. What is important for Kristeva is the transition from need to desire.[82] This experience of loss or absence Kristeva sees as a precondition for the development of language: "The emergence of the sign presumes the absence of the object, and so the acceptance of loss."[83] This experience of absence and loss now applies to Mary. She has experienced both the loss of her brother and a significant change in her relationship with Jesus; she now desires something beyond what she has wanted before, and the absence of that something fuels her movement toward language and subjectivity.

Her simple statement, uttered "without further explanatory comment to suggest that Jesus' presence may have saved her brother (v. 32), transcends Martha's aggressive understanding of Jesus as a miracle-worker and Messiah (vv. 21–2)."[84] Another difference that distinguishes the tone of the two sisters' utterances is the use of the possessive "my" (μου); it appears earlier in the sentence in Mary's statement, indicating a stronger connection with her brother and a more profound impact of his death on her.[85] Like Martha, Mary may believe in the power Jesus has over death, but the tone behind her words suggests that her belief is tinged with sorrow, confusion, and hurt. The loss that Mary has suffered—of her brother's life and of her earlier relationship with Jesus—is brought back to her when she utters the sentence. Her use of language is a way to recover what has been lost, as Kristeva explains:

---

81. McAfee, *Julia Kristeva*, 23; Oliver, *Reading Kristeva*, 93–98; Payne, *Reading Theory*, 171–78; Beardsworth, *Julia Kristeva*, 50.

82. Oliver, *Reading Kristeva*, 18, 31–32, 35.

83. Beardsworth, *Julia Kristeva*, 103.

84. Moloney, "Faith of Martha and Mary," 482–83; Moloney, "Can Everyone Be Wrong?," 516–17.

85. Van Tilborg, *Imaginative Love*, 193.

'I have lost an essential object that happens to be, in the final analysis, my mother,' is what the speaking being seems to be saying. 'But no, I have found her again in signs, or rather since I consent to lose her I have not lost her . . . I can recover her in language.'[86]

The Semiotic Dimension of Language

Martha's Partial Faith

We have seen that Martha is universally accepted by John scholars as the one who takes initiative, who goes out to meet Jesus, who proclaims her belief in his ability to work miracles by virtue of his relationship with God. But a closer reading of the text suggests a different interpretation of Martha's belief. Francis J. Moloney is one of a handful of commentators who sees in Martha an incomplete and imperfect faith. In analyzing her statements, he finds indications of partial understanding and limited vision.

First, Martha does not hesitate in professing her faith in Jesus as a worker of miracles; by virtue of his access to God, she believes that anything he asks will be granted. With this statement, Martha is linked to Nicodemus (3:2) and to the man born blind (9:31–33), both of whom believe that Jesus is able to work miracles because of his unique access to God.[87] But the text has already been critical of those who believe in Jesus because of the signs he does (in Jerusalem during Passover, 2:23; upon meeting Nathanael, 1:50; in conversation with Nicodemus, 3:2; and with the crowds beside the lake, 6:26); Martha repeats the misunderstanding of these characters who see Jesus as able to perform miracles because God is with him. When Jesus tries to correct Martha, saying, "Your brother will rise again" (11:23), she does not allow space for Jesus to elaborate before jumping in to say she knows that (Οἶδα ὅτι) "he will rise again in the resurrection on the last day" (11:24). Like others in her world, her beliefs are shaped by her history and culture, and she does not display openness to hearing something new. When Jesus again attempts to correct her, he does so by asking pointedly, "do you believe?" (11:26), presumably to focus her attention on the full truth of what he is saying.

Next, in Martha's well-known profession of faith ("Yes, Lord, I believe that you are the Messiah, the Son of God, the one coming into the

86. Kristeva, *Black Sun*, 43.
87. Moloney, *Signs and Shadows*, 160.

world"; 11:27), Moloney highlights the use of a verb in the perfect tense (πεπίστευκα), suggesting that Martha has *always* believed Jesus to be the fulfillment of her messianic expectations. In other words, nothing has changed in her understanding of Jesus as a result of her interaction with him, nor has she moved beyond her original faith.

Finally, Moloney points to the titles Martha employs for Jesus (messiah, son of God, the one coming into the world), arguing that first-century Jewish use of these expressions reflects "the limited faith of those who confess their belief in these terms." These same expressions also are used by Nicodemus ("a teacher who has come from God"; ἀπὸ θεοῦ ἐλήλυθας διδάσκαλος; 3:2) and the Samaritan woman ("Messiah . . . who is called Christ"; Μεσσίας ἔρχεται ὁ λεγόμενος Χριστός; 4:25), suggesting that like them, Martha has fallen short of authentic belief and reached only the stage of partial belief.[88] Martha's profession of faith reveals her groundedness in the Jewish faith; belief in a final resurrection is very much orthodox Pharisaism and, therefore, not exactly the unquestioning belief in Jesus as it first appears to be.[89]

Physical Life vs. Spiritual Life

In addition, the use of the verb "to live" (ζάω) in vv. 25 and 26 introduces the key Johannine theme of eternal life into this part of the narrative. When Jesus corrects Martha in her mistaken impression about resurrection on the last day, he clarifies that if believers die physically, they will continue to enjoy spiritual (eternal) life, and believers who are spiritually alive will never die spiritually. It is significant that Jesus says to Martha, "Those who believe in me, even though they die, will live, and everyone who lives and believes in me will never die" (11:25-26). Raymond Brown makes a compelling argument that, while the Johannine Jesus uses the same verb "to live" (ζάω) in both of these verses, he actually is making two distinct points: "the believer, if he dies physically, will live spiritually" (11:25) and "the believer who is alive spiritually will never die spiritually."[90] The physical life Jesus will restore to Lazarus, then, is not the same as spiritual life—eternal life or life from above. Brown makes the case for Lazarus being representative of

---

88. Moloney, "Can Everyone Be Wrong?," 513-14; Moloney, "Faith of Martha and Mary," 474-79.
89. Barrett, *John*, 328-29.
90. Brown, *John I-XII*, 425.

all those whom Jesus loves—that is, the new members of his community. He says, "Just as Jesus gives life to his beloved Lazarus, so will he give life to his beloved Christians."[91] This seeming contradiction suggests that Jesus' purpose in raising Lazarus will be not only to restore physical life to him, but also (and more importantly) to make spiritual life, life from above, possible for all.

This theme of spiritual life is expanded upon in the following verses. When Jesus asks where they have lain the body of Lazarus, it is Mary, along with the Judeans, who leads him there with the request, "Come and see" (ἔρχου καὶ ἴδε; 11:34). This is the same invitation Jesus issues to the first disciples and the same that Philip offers to Nathanael (1:39, 46). In all of these cases, this statement is an invitation to recognition and a response to the question (sometimes implicit), "What are you looking for?" (1:38). The verb "to seek" (ζητέω), which appears thirty-four times in John's gospel, amplifies the theme of seeking and finding that runs through the narrative. It describes the "disposition of those who come to belief, as well as the dispositions of the Father and of Jesus himself, who seeks out his own . . . The search is mutual, and the knowing and loving will be mutual."[92] As we will see, it is Mary, rather than Martha, who receives and offers the invitation to seek and to find.

Mary Weeps

There is an additional dimension of Mary's response to Jesus that also sets it apart from Martha's. After she speaks, Mary remains silent, and appears to be overcome with sorrow over her brother's death—illustrating Kristeva's claim that the symbolic can break down at "the inconsolable loss of a loved one."[93] Prior to this point, although Mary has been in grief, she also has been receptive and hopeful—moving out toward Jesus, hearing his voice, showing respect and openness, and trusting in his presence. Now she weeps.

What is markedly different about Mary's response to Jesus can be explained by Kristeva's understanding of the semiotic dimension of language. In *Revolution in Poetic Language*, Kristeva sets forth the idea of meaning—in written and spoken language—as emerging not only from the denotative dimensions of the words themselves but also from the affective, emotive,

---

91. Ibid., 431.
92. Culbertson, *Poetics of Revelation*, 158.
93. Keltner, *Kristeva: Thresholds*, 56.

and poetic elements as well. Within what she calls the "signifying process," Kristeva distinguishes two elements of language, thus attributing to signification a "layering" of meanings from both conscious and unconscious realms. She distinguishes the "symbolic" modality of language—a clear and logical expression of the speaker's meaning expressed by the words themselves—from the "semiotic," the expression or "emotional traces" of the subject's feelings, desires, or drives. The symbolic dimension of signification, which derives from the language system itself and is subject to the rules of grammar and syntax, uses mutually accepted signs and makes it possible for listeners to recognize the speaker's references to ideas, objects, and events. The semiotic, on the other hand, is the "hidden" element of meaning that gives energy, depth, and feeling to the symbolic level of language. It is associated with the unconscious modes of expression, and can include cries, laughter, sound, touch, gesture, smiles, rhythms, intonation. These two elements are never separate, working together, intertwined in much the same way as body and mind, feeling and reason, unconscious and conscious. Kristeva argues that both dimensions are essential for meaning; without the symbolic, significance is indecipherable and without sense, and without the semiotic, it is without energy and emotion.[94]

Kristeva's theories help us understand the ways in which an individual's unconscious drives find their way into language through nonverbal signifying systems. By illustrating how a type of signification, the semiotic, already is operating in the individual before the acquisition of formal language, Kristeva recognizes the body as an essential element in human discourse. Unconscious bodily drives, represented by the rhythm of speech, tone of voice, and movement of the body, give substance, importance, and meaning to language. Semiotic activity is the result of these bodily drives. For Kristeva, the transition from the semiotic realm to the symbolic must be understood as both bodily and social, and these instinctual drives form a "bridge between the biological foundation of signifying functioning and its determination by the family and society."[95]

---

94. Kristeva, *Revolution in Poetic Language*, 3–4, 23–24; McAfee, *Julia Kristeva*, 13–18; Kristeva, *In the Beginning*, 5–7.

95. Kristeva, *Revolution in Poetic Language*, 167, 25–27. Kristeva has been challenged by feminist scholars such as Judith Butler for associating the semiotic with the maternal and the symbolic with the paternal. In dividing these categories along gender lines, Butler claims, Kristeva has preserved the idea of culture as a masculine construct while essentializing the feminine as a pre-symbolic and "pre-cultural reality"—one that is automatically subordinate to the symbolic (masculine, logical) realm of language and

With her unique understanding of the signifying process, Kristeva attends to the affects or "emotional traces" that exist between speaker and listener. It is through this concept of semiotic and symbolic domains that Kristeva is able to hold together "word" and "flesh." In fact, Kristeva argues that *without* the incursion of the semiotic (drives) into the symbolic (signifier), the person herself becomes only a sign.[96]

> These two modalities (the semiotic and the symbolic) are inseparable within the *signifying* process that constitutes language, and the dialectic between them determines the type of discourse (narrative, meta-language, theory, poetry, etc.) involved; in other words, so-called "natural" language allows for different modes of articulation of the semiotic and the symbolic . . . Because the subject is always *both* semiotic *and* symbolic, no signifying system that produces can be either "exclusively" semiotic or "exclusively" symbolic, and is instead necessarily marked by an indebtedness to both.[97]

Kristeva's insistence on the need for both the symbolic and semiotic dimensions of language illustrates why Mary's response to Jesus has more impact than Martha's intellectual statement of faith. Mary's comment is very much embodied as she expresses her feelings physically—kneeling at Jesus' feet and weeping as the emotions she feels pour out from her. In Mary, the semiotic and symbolic come together; in Martha's comments, there is only the symbolic—without energy, emotion, or aliveness.

Mary's Response as Subversive

In addition, Mary's response—which is more complete, authentic, and embodied than Martha's—appears to have an impact on Jesus as well. She has "broken through" something in him, provoking a reaction. Kristeva explains that, while both the symbolic and the semiotic are essential for signification to have meaning, she also points out that the semiotic "disrupts" the symbolic, breaking through the logic and rationality of its signification

---

culture. Butler, "Body Politics," 104–11. Kristeva would argue that neither the semiotic nor the symbolic is subordinate to the other; instead, both are indispensible to language and work together to create meaning.

96. McAfee, *Julia Kristeva*, 14–18; Kristeva, *In the Beginning*, 5–7; Oliver, *Reading Kristeva*, 33.

97. Kristeva, *Revolution in Poetic Language*, 92–93.

to reveal unconscious drives and desires.[98] The semiotic, as Kristeva makes clear in *Revolution in Poetic Language*, is evidenced in creative expression (music, art, literature, and poetry) and religion; it is the expression of the unconscious before being put into symbolic language, before being "repressed" in a culturally-accepted signifying system. The symbolic "is the language of transparency, power and conformity, and, as such, is aligned with patriarchal functions in culture—*le non/nom de père*—which signals the father's name and the father's prohibitions in social and psychic formations."[99] The semiotic, on the other hand, is "pre-linguistic" and can be found not only in the infant child's utterances, but also in creative expressions, and in everyday discourse as well. While conventional wisdom suggests that it is necessary to "contain" these passions or "excesses" because they disrupt the order and logic of language, Kristeva argues that it is precisely these elements that give meaning to language.[100]

Understanding the semiotic as a type of subversion informs our understanding of Mary's progression in the story. Mary goes beyond the accepted norms of behavior in her weeping and kneeling before Jesus, and these expressions have the effect of subversion. While her sister fulfills, and perhaps mimics, the expectations of a good disciple and a faithful believer, Mary moves past these expectations and responds authentically. Her semiotic displacements help to overcome not only the repressive patriarchal code of behavior for women, but also any pre-determined notions of what it means to be faithful to Jesus. She makes clear what is most important and, in doing so, subverts the norms of power and authority in her world. As she transgresses these borders, turning away from the logic of patriarchy, of Judaism, and breaking the law-driven symbolic order, she turns toward an entirely new way of being.

Mary as "the Subject on Trial"

As we have already seen, becoming a subject for Kristeva is not something that happens only in infancy; it is an ongoing dynamic process that occurs throughout the life span. Kristeva makes the point that subjectivity is never stable or fixed; instead through a variety of experiences, events, and interactions, an individual's selfhood is continuously being shaped and

98. Ibid., 70, 81.
99. Robbins, *Literary Feminisms*, 128.
100. Kristeva, *Revolution in Poetic Language*, 68–71; McAfee, *Julia Kristeva*, 15.

reshaped. The person, then, is a subject-in-process (*le sujet en procès*). We can see that Mary is in process, continuously being formed as a subject as she moves through the process of being born from above. But, we also recall that Kristeva understands subjectivity and language as inextricably linked, insisting that the signifying process must encompass the subject himself, his ongoing formation, and his bodily, unconscious, and social relations. For this reason, the phrase *le sujet en procès* has another meaning for Kristeva: "the subject on trial." By this, Kristeva refers to the transgressive nature of the signifying process, particularly the semiotic modality that disrupts the accepted, orderly means of communication. As she critiques the "capitalist mode of production" in language, a system that represses the *process* through which meaning is produced and focuses solely on the artifacts of language such as "empirical evidence, a systematizable given, and an observable object"—Kristeva highlights the semiotic mode that expresses unconscious drives and reveals important changes in the subject.[101] Mary is a "subject on trial," in the sense that her discourse breaks through the accepted norms and becomes a subversive act. While Martha's is the more accepted mode of language production, Mary's language disrupts established patterns and reveals significant changes she is experiencing as she moves toward rebirth.

---

101. Kristeva, *Revolution in Poetic Language*, 13–16. In her psychoanalytic and language theory, Kristeva seeks to address the metaphysical question of origins: does the "Word" really come first in the process of humans becoming speaking, social beings? Her argument is that Western thought reveals a "logocentric" bias, in its claim that the "Word" is the distinguishing characteristic of humans and the beginning of all things; what most consider "origins," she considers heterogeneity vis-à-vis language. She repeatedly counters John's opening verse, "In the beginning was the Word" with her own version, such as "in the beginning was love" or "in the beginning was suffering." Pollock, "Dialogue with Julia Kristeva," 8–9. Kristeva seeks to dismantle the logocentric narrative, and she does so primarily through her discourse on the semiotic dimension of language, in which she tries to recover the pre-verbal foundation of the human subject. She wants to recapture what has traditionally been considered unnamable (semiotic expressions of emotions, sensations, drives, and affects) and she urges a return to this "underlying but forgotten causality of language and the subject." Margaroni, "Lost Foundation," 80–81.

The Mirror Stage

Jesus Weeps

At the end of the passage, something extraordinary occurs. Jesus sees that Mary and her friends are weeping, and he is moved to tears as well (11:35). The verb used to describe Mary's weeping (κλαίω; 11:33), which can be translated as "lamenting," "bewailing," or "mourning for," has a slightly different connotation from the verb describing Jesus' weeping (δακρύω; 11:35), most commonly understood to mean simply "shedding tears" or "weeping."[102] As Culpepper reminds us, ch. 11 has more indications of Jesus' emotions than any other chapter in John's gospel, emotions that culminate in an intensity that is striking compared to the relative aloofness we see in him throughout the rest of John's narrative.[103] Some commentators propose that Jesus responds to the two sisters based on their different personalities; with Martha, the more thinking and practical of the two, he has an intellectual discussion about theological issues and, with Mary, the more emotional sister, he reveals his empathy and grief.[104] What is significant is that Jesus does not diminish Mary's grief; in fact, when he cries, he affirms the most universal human experience of sorrow in the face of death. Yet, there is more going on here than Jesus adapting his response to each sister.

There is no scholarly consensus as to the proper interpretation of Jesus' earlier reaction in v. 33b: "he was greatly disturbed in spirit and deeply moved" (ἐνεβριμήσατο τῷ πνεύματι καὶ ἐτάραξεν ἑαυτόν). Modern commentators offer translations such as "to groan," "to sigh," "to chafe," "to be strongly moved" or "to be troubled," or "to cause inward turmoil."[105] Traditional interpreters such as Bultmann and Schnackenburg consider it to be an indication of anger at the unbelief of Mary and the Jews, a "lack of faith in his ability to raise the dead."[106] Brown proposes that, in this scene, Jesus is angry at the power of death that he sees as the work of Satan.[107] Schneiders interprets Jesus' emotion here as anger over the mourners' failure to understand that, although human death is a reality, it serves God's purpose

---

102. Danker, *Greek-English Lexicon*, 545, 211.
103. Culpepper, *Anatomy of the Fourth Gospel*, 110.
104. Kitzberger, "Mary of Bethany," 578.
105. Danker, *Greek-English Lexicon*, 322, 990.
106 Bultmann, *John*, 406; Schnackenburg, *John*, 2:336.
107 Brown, *John I–XII*, 435.

of bringing believers into union with God.[108] These explanations appear to contradict Jesus' earlier reaction to Martha's glib and too-easy expression of faith; would he expect these mourners to automatically understand not only the powers he has been granted by God or the ultimate meaning of human death? For other scholars, Jesus' response is an indication of his grief over the death of his friend and his own impending fate; Jesus again feels strong emotions as he nears the tomb (11:38) and when he contemplates his own death (12:27). John's use of verbs allows for different interpretations but, especially when considered in the context of his weeping directly before this statement (v. 35), Culpepper contends that Jesus is expressing grief over what he is about to do—restore life to Lazarus—because he knows it will be the precipitating factor in his own death.[109]

Whether his weeping with Mary relates to the death of his friend or his own impending fate, Jesus expresses deep emotion for what is a very real human loss. I agree with Moloney in his reading of Jesus' tears, and his subsequent emotional response of anger, as an acknowledgment of what Jesus understands as a "profound human experience" and "the grief of his living friends, even though he knew that grief to be unnecessary, and that his raising of Lazarus was a response to his dawning perception of the depth of human despair, a depth he must 'sound' even though he recognizes that it is due to a 'misperception.'"[110] Suffering is a very real human experience, and Jesus reveals his understanding of it in his emotional response to Mary.

Mary's Reflected Humanity

The response Mary has provoked in Jesus calls to mind Lacan's mirror stage, which is simultaneous with the thetic break. During this stage, as the child sees itself reflected in the mirror, another phenomenon occurs: the child looking in the mirror eventually recognizes that its self is somehow reflected there. While the child experiences the image as whole and complete, it does not recognize that its actual self is immature, fragmented, and incomplete. Lacan calls this the "desire of the Other." As the child's desire moves to the other side of the mirror, the child assimilates herself into that body and ultimately recognizes herself as a body. The child then realizes that she is separate from the rest of the world and from her mother,

108. Schneiders, "Death in the Community," 51.
109 Culpepper, *Anatomy of the Fourth Gospel*, 111.
110. Moloney, "Can Everyone Be Wrong?," 518 n. 44.

the protective environment in which she has existed. Eventually, after the mirror stage, the mother takes the place of the Other in the mirror as the child fully recognizes her as another being. The child is ultimately unified "through its doubling in the mirror . . . it must become two in order to become one (a unified self)."[111]

Lacan proposes that the function of the mirror stage is to establish a relationship between the developing subject and its outer reality. When the child identifies an image in the mirror, a transformation takes place. It is precisely the gap between the developing subject's ideal "I" and actual "I" that gives rise to subjectivity. By representing an ideal unified image (in comparison to the fragmentation the child actually experiences), "the *imago* is a captivation of the subject, transforming it."[112] In weeping after she weeps, Jesus "mirrors" for Mary what she is becoming, standing in for her and preparing her for entry into a larger, alternative world and a new reality. While Mary's subjectivity and self are still fragmented, Jesus reflects back an image of what she is to become.

Lacan contends that the developing child enters the symbolic realm and becomes a subject precisely at the time of the mirror stage; prior to this time, the child has a fragmented self and no unified sense of experience. But Kristeva argues that the development of subjectivity and language is ongoing—present before this stage as the child exists in the semiotic *chora* and present after as the child moves more and more into the symbolic realm. For Kristeva, it is precisely the semiotic drives and the articulation of these drives that move the not-yet-subject toward the thetic break and position the child for the entry into subjectivity.

Mary Moves toward a New Reality

When we look at Mary's actions throughout this part of the narrative, it is clear that there is more happening than a superficial reading of the text would suggest. Mary's actions recall Kristeva's contention that there is a back-and-forth movement between the semiotic and the symbolic, a process in which the child's instinctual drives increasingly become organized according to the laws of society and nature. Operating in this process is a phenomenon Kristeva calls "rejection" (or negativity), in which the child separates or discharges matter. Periods of stasis follow this material

111. Oliver, *Reading Kristeva*, 20, 37.
112. Beardsworth, *Julia Kristeva*, 37–38.

rejection, and it is the oscillation between these two states that produces something new and eventually propels the child into subjectivity. Kristeva details the "logic of renewal" that occurs within the development of subjectivity as: "rejection—stasis—rejection—stasis (etc.)—thesis—rejection —stasis."[113] If we interpret Mary's actions in light of Kristeva's pattern of rejection and stasis, we can see the movement she makes in this section of the narrative. In each of the instances of rejection that Mary experiences, she is separated (or separates herself) from someone close to her; in each instance of stasis, she reaches a plateau where something new is created within her. The pattern can be summarized as follows:

1. Mary's brother falls ill—*rejection*
2. The sisters send word to Jesus—*stasis*
3. Jesus does not respond/her brother dies—*rejection*
4. She carries on with prayer and mourning—*stasis*
5. She does not go out to meet Jesus when he arrives—*rejection*
6. Jesus calls her; she goes out to meet him—*stasis*
7. She tells him of her disappointment—*thesis (the thetic break)*
8. She cries—*rejection*
9. Jesus cries; she leads him to the tomb—*stasis*

This dynamic and oscillating movement is an example of Kristeva's theory of the subject in process, a subject who is continuously being shaped by the relational forces in her life.

Conclusion

Like the developing child who exists in the safety of the semiotic *chora*, Mary exists in an environment of relative safety and comfort at the beginning of her story. As she experiences the death of her brother and begins to see that the union with Jesus she thought she had is not real, she moves from security to awakening.

This stage is analogous to the Johannine concept of blindness or "living in the world below." The evangelist offers a picture of the human condition

---

113. Oliver, *Reading Kristeva*, 19–22, 41–47; Kristeva, *Revolution in Poetic Language*, 172.

as one of separation from the divine realm; through complementary statements such as "You are from below, I am from above; you are of this world, I am not of this world" (8:23), we learn that human beings are cut off from Jesus himself and from God, the very source of life. And this separation is of our own making, caused by our inability to see the reality Jesus represents: "This is the Spirit of truth, whom the world cannot receive, because it neither sees him nor knows him" (14:17). As human beings are immersed in the "things" of the world—wealth, power, status, honor, health—they believe those to be real and true. Forgetting they are part of God's creation, ignoring the truth of their own dependence on the one who bestows life, humans believe they can provide for themselves the security they need in order to exist. There is an illusion of oneness, but humans actually are separated from God and blind to the true reality offered by Jesus.

In Mary's story, she is forced by an external event to leave the safety of her environment; a disruption occurs that forces her to re-evaluate her life, her identity, her relationship with Jesus. And it is this event that moves her forward on the journey.

3

The Boundary of Transformation

JOHN 11:38–45

Introduction

Most commentators consider the raising of Lazarus to be the pivotal point in John's gospel, the final sign in the Book of Signs and the triggering event in the plot to kill Jesus. Yet the miracle is narrated in just eight verses. After Mary and the Jews lead Jesus to the tomb, we note that he, again "greatly disturbed," proceeds to where Lazarus has been laid, ordering that the stone be taken away. Martha protests, telling Jesus that the corpse is now four days old. Jesus reminds her that he already said that she would see the glory of God, and the stone is removed. Jesus offers an audible prayer, and calls to Lazarus to come out. Lazarus emerges wrapped in strips of cloth, and Jesus orders that he be unbound and let go. Finally, some of the Judeans who were there with Mary come to believe in Jesus.

There is no question that Mary is present for the miracle Jesus performs, because she and the Judeans lead Jesus there and because the text tells us that "Many of the Jews therefore, who had come with Mary and had seen what Jesus did, believed in him" (11:45). Yet the text tells us nothing about Mary's reaction to this event. For this reason, reading the passage from the perspective of Mary's journey toward subjectivity requires a different kind of reading strategy. In order to infer Mary's response in this part of the story, I call upon Iser's well-known notion of filling in textual "gaps." For Iser, what draws readers into a text and engages their full participation in the reading process are significant gaps—usually in information about events, motives, characters, plot—that require readers to construct meaning. Because texts cannot possibly convey the perspectives of all characters at the same time (and this is especially true of John's gospel), the reader must create connections, filling in the gaps in the narrative. Iser is clear that these absences are necessary not only to create interest in a story, but also to engage the reader's imagination.[1] The gaps are not arbitrary, however; they are something that disrupts the continuity of a narrative, something vitally important to the story that is suspended.[2]

Meir Sternberg elaborates on the value of these absences in biblical studies: to lead the reader "from the truth to the whole truth."[3] Sternberg also highlights several reasons for the relevance of suspense in the Bible. First, gaps in the telling of a story are in accordance with real life, since even an omniscient narrator cannot be expected to know all things at once. Second, suspense has moral value in the sense of giving the reader an "epistemological dividend" when the fate of a character is ultimately revealed. Sternberg maintains that a gap is "contrived by temporal displacement," and by this he means that often the missing piece is given at some point earlier or later in the narrative.[4]

Out of all the gospels, John is the one most known for a "broken narrative style," featuring gaps and riddles that encourage the reader to search for a deeper meaning.[5] Iser's reading strategy is especially useful for reading Mary's story since we have details about her before and after the raising of Lazarus and—as we will see in the following chapter—it is clear that something significant happens to her in the intervening time. So we must fill in the gaps based on textual details in the scenes prior to and following the miracle scene. In this case, the absence of information about Mary in this scene serves to create a greater impact when we finally see evidence of the change she has undergone.

---

1. Iser, *Reading Process*, 213.
2. Iser, *Implied Reader*, 33; Iser, *Act of Reading*, 124.
3. Sternberg, *Poetics of Biblical Narrative*, 235.
4. Ibid., 235, 265–66.
5. Zimmerman, "Narrative Hermeneutics," 82–83.

The Developing Subject

As we enter the scene of the raising of Lazarus, we can imagine that Mary has been in the process of moving away from Jesus, aware that her relationship with him must change and already *has* changed, but still hopeful that ultimately he will not disappoint or abandon her. In this liminal space, she stands between the world she has known and the new reality she is about to discover. Like an infant who is between the world of the semiotic *chora* and the larger world of the symbolic order, the dimensions of Mary's world have been limited, but a different reality will be revealed to her as she moves closer to becoming an independent subject.

Mary Leads Jesus to the Tomb

All of Mary's actions to this point have been characteristic of an ordinary human response to grief: denial, isolation, anger, bargaining, and sorrow, but as she leads Jesus to her brother's grave, we can intuit a deeper dimension of her experience that sets her apart from other characters in the story. While we see Martha continuously engaged in external actions, Mary remains inwardly-focused. Recall that, in the earlier scene, we see Mary at home with a small group of Judeans, in the traditional posture of a mourner and—because the evangelist does not use explicit words for prayer but suggests it through various postures "to preserve a sense of prayer's ultimate indefinability,"[6]—it is not unreasonable to assume that she is praying.

The same contrast between the two sisters in terms of inner and outer orientation appears in the raising-of-Lazarus scene. Here, Martha reveals her limited understanding, going so far as to warn Jesus that he should not go near the tomb (11:39):

> Martha expresses not false sincerity but real doubt. She balks at Jesus' order to remove the stone from Lazarus' tomb, sure that his body has begun to decompose. Whatever belief Mary may have arrived at with πεπίστευκα seems either to have evaporated quickly or never to have been as firm as she thought it to be.[7]

In contrast, Mary is silent, but her greater receptivity is implied since she is the one who has led Jesus to the tomb. It appears as if Martha, however,

---

6. Brodie, *John*, 60.
7. Maccini, *Her Testimony is True*, 156.

wants to hold tight to what she already (mis)understands; her words to Jesus suggest that she is experiencing doubt about whether Jesus is able to help after such a long time—so much so that he must remind her to trust that she will see the glory of God (11:40). In contrast, Mary's silence suggests humility and a deeper receptivity to the events that are to follow.

An inward attitude of prayer, much like we see in Jesus at various points in John's gospel, suggests that Mary has an inner inclination toward God that Martha and the others, for all their efforts to please Jesus, do not exhibit. What is the origin of this inner drive? On several occasions, we have heard Jesus talk about believers being "drawn" or "taught" by God: "No one can come to me unless drawn by the Father who sent me . . ." and "Everyone who has heard and learned from the Father comes to me" (6:44–45).[8] Given the trajectory of Mary's story so far, it is likely that she is beginning to sense such a "draw" or "call" from God the Father. We see evidence of this in her prayerful attitude, her humility, her openness and receptivity, her respect for Jesus. This is indicative of a growing awareness in her that something more awaits.

In Kristeva's understanding, the developing subject likewise experiences an innate desire. We know that an infant's early move toward symbolic language only occurs when she senses absence or lack. Kristeva expands on this idea and, although she parts ways with Lacan in several areas, here she agrees with him that, in the move toward subjectivity, the child increasingly experiences a gap between needs and satisfaction. What the infant really wants is the mother's constant love and automatic response to her needs, neither of which is possible. And, since it is only through sensing *lack* that language and subjectivity are attained, "the subject is always the subject of desire."[9] Kristeva argues that the abjection of the mother—all abjection, "is in fact the recognition of the *want* on which any being, meaning, language, or desire is founded."[10] But she goes even further in describing abjection as a mourning for something "that has always already been lost."[11] Kristeva also suggests that the child's "want, loss, emptiness—all signal the impact of alterity at the very beginnings of subject constitution."[12] For Mary as developing subject, the emptiness she experiences as a result of her separa-

---

8. Thompson, "Raising of Lazarus," 242.
9. McAfee, *Julia Kristeva*, 34.
10. Kristeva, *Powers of Horror*, 5; Keltner, *Kristeva: Thresholds*, 52.
11. Kristeva, *Powers of Horror*, 15.
12. Keltner, *Kristeva: Thresholds*, 52.

tion from Jesus is a sign that there is a beyond, a "something other" that is outside her comprehension but to which she is nevertheless drawn.

The Separate-but-Supportive Maternal Figure

Jesus' Role in Mary's Rebirth

Although there are hints that Mary has an inner desire that propels her toward rebirth, she is not able to accomplish this on her own: "however oriented people may naturally be toward the divine realm, however deep their longing, there is within them a darkness or dividedness, with the result that they cannot immediately connect with their God."[13] Similarly, Kristeva insists that, even though the developing subject possesses an innate faculty for individuation and symbolization, the parent figure must activate this natural competency: "The newborn responds not so much to a natural programming but to parental wish for what the child will be."[14]

Jesus holds a vision for what Mary can become, and his role at this point in her journey of rebirth is to activate her movement toward subjectivity. But Kristeva reminds us that the process of "subjectivation" is successful only to the extent that the maternal figure is able to facilitate separation; without appropriate separation, the developing child will confuse fantasy and reality. The maternal agency eases the loss the child feels in separating by holding and providing supportive "containment" for her.[15] In Mary's pre-subject stage, Jesus—as the semiotic *chora*/maternal agency—has facilitated her development by allowing her to feel the full impact of her grief but also by listening, being present, and mirroring her feelings—allowing her to separate but "containing" her at the same time.

The Son's Oneness with the Father

Now, at Lazarus' tomb, Jesus shares with Mary and the others present a glimpse of his intimacy and oneness with the Father. In this scene, as in others, Jesus interrupts the action to pray: he "looked upwards and said . . ." (11: 41–42). This gesture is an attitude of prayer similar to what we see when Jesus prays for his disciples in the farewell discourse: "After Jesus had

13. Brodie, *John*, 56.
14. Gambaudo, *Kristeva, Psychoanalysis and Culture*, 139.
15. Ibid., 112, 140.

spoken these words, he looked up to heaven" (17:1). What is interesting about the prayer at the tomb, however, is that Jesus does not petition God for help; rather, it is an offering of thanksgiving in advance, given in the sure knowledge that whatever he asks will be granted.[16] On one level, the tone and words of the prayer serve to underscore Jesus' intimacy and Sonship with God the Father.

But, on a deeper level, the prayer illustrates another truth announced earlier: "Indeed, just as the Father raises the dead and gives them life, so also the Son gives life to whomever he wishes" (5:21; also 5:25, 28). The prayer alerts listeners to the fact that Jesus the Son works continuously with the Father, but is obedient to him, as he reproduces the actions of God: "Very truly, I tell you, the Son can do nothing on his own, but only what he sees the Father doing; for whatever the Father does, the Son does likewise" (5:19).[17] The reason Jesus does the works of the Father, he explains, is so that people will know that "the Father is in me and I am in the Father" (10:38).[18] Even before the miracle Jesus performs in the raising of Lazarus, then, the prayer at the tomb clearly establishes the oneness that exists between Jesus the Son and God the Father.

Throughout the John narrative, Jesus alludes to the relationship he shares with the Father and to the possibility of believers sharing in that same abiding unity: "As you, Father, are in me and I am in you, may they also be in us" (17:21; also 17:11b; 22–23; 26). But if Jesus and the Father are one, we must wonder why it is necessary for him to enter a state of prayer, especially if "he continually stands before God as the asker and therefore as the receiver."[19] We can read a secondary purpose in Jesus' saying the prayer aloud: he is modeling for believers a relationship of dependence, but one characterized by love, intimacy, mutuality, and abiding unity. He is showing Mary and the other onlookers what it means to be in an authentic relationship of loving unity with God the Father.

Jesus' Love for the Father

Mary no doubt witnesses Jesus' love, intimacy, and oneness with the Father in this scene. And, as a developing subject, she may have conflicting

16. Lincoln, "Lazarus Story," 221.
17. Barrett, *John*, 60, 322, 336.
18. Lincoln, "Lazarus Story," 218.
19. Bultmann, *John*, 408.

feelings about what she sees—continuing sadness over what she perceives as a loss of Jesus' love *and* a longing to experience the obvious love he feels for the Father. Kristeva tells us that one of the ways a newborn child attempts to keep the mother's interest is by positioning herself in the space of the mother's desire, usually the father whom the mother loves. As the child senses the mother's desire for something other than her, she moves toward what the mother loves in an attempt to close the gap, and "the object of maternal desire is what the child will thrive to become."[20]

Initially, the developing child's illusory experiences of a father as someone other than her, a "not I," allows her to identify "with the paternal function as it already exists in the mother," thereby providing a replacement for the child's dependence on the actual maternal body.[21] We see a similar pattern in Mary, as she witnesses Jesus' love for the Father, the "Other" he loves. Jesus intentionally reveals his intimate relationship with the Father, and although Mary does not yet have a direct experience of God, she begins to have a vision of this emerging paternal image as it is already present in Jesus. This sets up a space within her to enter into unity with the Father when she later encounters God's presence herself. The space created by this "not I" in the child is the space that ultimately will be filled by the structure of language and the Father of the Law. For Mary, instead of leading to the Father of the Law, however, as it does in Kristeva's construct, the opened space will be filled with an abiding unity with both Jesus and God the Father—integrating the maternal and paternal functions to bring wholeness. For now, Mary has the support to let go of her less-than-mature relationship with Jesus for an ultimately more satisfying relationship with Jesus and God. This in and of itself is a move toward subjectivity, as it is with a developing child who trades a dyadic dependence and identification with the maternal body for a triadic identification with the mother and the object of her desire.[22]

20. Gambaudo, *Kristeva*, 139.
21. Oliver, *Reading Kristeva*, 79.
22. Ibid., 80–82.

The Imaginary Father

God as the Loving Imaginary Father

Mary's emerging interest in Jesus' love for the Father calls to mind what Kristeva terms the "loving imaginary father." To make this connection, we must return momentarily to the concept of the narcissistic structure—the psychic space in the developing child that Kristeva sees as critical for the emergence of subjectivity and the possibility of symbolic language. In her detailed analysis of the pre-subject stages, Kristeva credits the narcissistic structure with activating the child's abjection of the maternal body; helping the child cope with the ensuing loss; offsetting the gap between the image the child sees in the mirror and the actual fragmented body as she experiences it; and setting up the move toward symbolic language. Also occurring within this structure is the loving imaginary father.[23]

Kristeva's notion of the loving father is in direct response to Freud and Lacan's father-centered theories that identify fear as the child's motivation for moving toward the symbolic realm. Kristeva refuses to accept fear as a motivator, arguing instead that abjection is what propels the child to the next stage. She also insists that separation from the mother, although painful, is pleasurable for the child because of love she feels from an idealized father figure, "an imaginary agent of love that allows the child to negotiate the passage between the maternal body and the Symbolic order."[24] Without the promise of this love, Kristeva argues, the developing child would not have a good enough reason to leave the safety of the maternal body. We will recall, however, that the child does not completely abandon the maternal figure; not only is the maternal agency still present in the abject that remains with the child, but also it is part of a the conglomerate mother-father figure that is Kristeva's imaginary father. Even as the child is separating from the mother, this vision of the loving father provides support—and

---

23. Oliver, "Crisis of Meaning," 40, 45–46. Oliver, *Reading Kristeva*, 78. Kristeva makes it clear that the father figure is *not* necessary a male, nor is it the Phallus or Lacan's Law of the Father. It is a vision of a loving figure, one that breaks up the child-mother dyad and helps the developing subject sever its dependence on the maternal body. Kristeva builds on Freud's idea of "the father of individual prehistory," but while he emphasizes the "sternness" of the father, she focuses on the nurturing and loving dimensions of the paternal figure. Gambaudo, *Kristeva*, 24.

24. Kristeva, *Tales of Love*, 33–34, 41–42; Oliver, *Reading Kristeva*, 69–72, 85–86.

both are critical to the emergence of subjectivity: "the maternal and paternal functions are two moments of birth of the human subject."[25]

Mary's shifting relationship with Jesus bears several similarities to the developing subject's vision of a loving father. First, in Mary's case, the image of a loving father compensates for the emptiness she experiences as a result of her losses, mediating the separation and facilitating her transition to a broader reality. More specifically, the vision of a loving father gives Mary an image of another presence, someone other than Jesus to identify with and place her hopes in. We know that in the process of detaching from a dyadic relationship with the mother, the developing child looks toward the object of the mother's desire—the father of the child, the mother's own father, or anyone who is symbolically Other. Kristeva argues for the absolute necessity of this Other to spark individuation, someone who plays the role of a third party to break up the mother-child dyad.[26] If all goes well, the infant begins to bind with the third party, a process Kristeva refers to as "primary identification." Through this bond, the child begins to see the third as a sort of model, and slowly begins to imitate the speech of that person, not yet as language but as repetition. As the child continues to separate from the maternal figure, she begins to idealize the father figure, and the foundation for language and meaning is conditioned. The child's emerging identity is transferred to this Other, and the subject is able to "become like him: One ... through love."[27]

Second, and most importantly, the image of a loving father exposes Mary to "exteriority," something outside and beyond her, but this presence appears as loving and nourishing.[28] This may not be Mary's first exposure to Otherness but, rather than being a threatening presence, in this case:

> It is the gift of an Other that puts loving idealization at the heart of ego formation, a loving idealization, then, that inscribes the alterity of this ... other at the core of the self. Since this alterity is

25. Gambaudo, *Kristeva*, 23.

26. Kristeva and Malcomson, "Foreign Body," 181–82. Kristeva herself suggests that the imaginary father, operating as a third party from beyond the mother and child, is comparable to the figure of God in the Christian tradition. She sees the trust involved in the relationship between the child and the imaginary father comparable to religious faith in the Christian God, which she defines as a "primary identification with a loving and protective agency." Kristeva, *New Maladies of the Soul*, 121–23, 179–80; Kristeva, *In the Beginning*, 124; Kristeva, *Tales of Love*, 40–41.

27. Kristeva, *Tales of Love*, 26; Keltner, *Kristeva: Thresholds*, 51.

28. Keltner, *Kristeva: Thresholds*, 51.

always potential alterity, it carries the subject toward the symbolic and others without compromising its autonomy in the journey.[29]

Ideally, as Mary completes her journey of being born from above, she will embrace this Otherness as part of her developing selfhood but not lose her individuality in the process.

The Subject-Father Relationship

As Jesus performs the raising of Lazarus, Mary's vision of the one Jesus loves begins to mature. And, in witnessing the miracle, she undergoes several changes in her emerging relationship with God the Father.

Purifying: Jesus Undoes Abjection, Defilement, and Estrangement

Recall that Mary's close contact with death has made her subject to the same conditions as her brother—the actual deceased person. Lazarus is the "abject," but Mary has experienced the abjection of death. Just as her brother's corpse is the ultimate in defilement, Mary is considered defiled as well. In this state of defilement, Mary experiences estrangement from God; similarly, Lazarus' death is the utmost of desacralization and separation from God. Finally, Lazarus physically has ceased to exist, and the condition of *tum'ah* also has rendered Mary emotionally lifeless; it is if she also is dead.[30] As we will see, in raising Lazarus from the tomb, Jesus reverses every one of these conditions not only in Lazarus, but also in Mary.

Because death—especially a corpse—represents the epitome of desacralization and estrangement from God, Mary is suspended between death and defilement on one hand and life and sanctity on the other.[31] Kristeva explains this as the abjected object standing on the border between human existence on one hand, and sacred order on the other.[32] She understands defilement in religious traditions, in fact, as "a social symbolic articulation of abjection, raising its dynamic of repulsion to the ritual level."[33]

---

29. Beardsworth, *Julia Kristeva*, 281 n. 10.
30. Feldman, *Biblical and Post-Biblical Defilement*, 93.
31. Ibid., 68–69.
32. Kristeva, *Powers of Horror*, 73.
33. Beardsworth, *Julia Kristeva*, 124.

Kristeva also highlights the fact that the foundation for much of the Judeo-Christian tradition involves purification rituals; many of the biblical stories involve individuals being abjected or needing to be cleansed. In Kristeva's view, it is only through purification rituals that an individual is set free from an innate impurity, and the proper social order is restored. Because defilement represents an incursion of the semiotic into the accepted symbolic and social order, purification rites shift the border by revealing "the boundary between semiotic authority and symbolic law."[34] In raising Lazarus, Jesus performs a purification ritual, one that "undoes" the experience of abjection, removes the impurity of death, and resolves both Lazarus' and Mary's estrangement from God. As a result, "a spiritually dead individual is won back into fellowship with God."[35] Although Mary has been temporarily estranged from herself, from her community, and from God, there are now no obstacles to the life of abiding unity to which Jesus invites her.

Sanctifying: Jesus Restores and Sanctifies Life

The raising of Lazarus also functions as a ritual of sanctification. We have heard Jesus talk about sanctifying the disciples and himself, "Sanctify them in the truth ... And for their sakes I sanctify myself" (17:17–19), and here he sanctifies both Lazarus and, by association, Mary. We know that to sanctify something is to set it apart for God, to move something from one world to another world, the world of the sacred. Bruce Malina points to a liminal space in this process, "the area of anxiety and concern as well as of joy and emotional highs, the area of interaction, the margin or borderline."[36] There is evidence of this marginal or borderline space in Jesus' movements prior to the miracle scene. We first see him outside of Judea (11:1–16), then he moves to a location outside of Bethany (11:17–37); and finally to the tomb itself (11:38–44)—"the spatial and ideological center of John 11."[37] We also know that the Jerusalem Temple is arranged in similar fashion, with a general assembly place, an intermediate interaction space, and the Holy of Holies.[38] Jesus' movement inward, then, replicates the arrangement of the

---

34. Kristeva, *Powers of Horror*, 73.
35. Story, "Mental Attitude of Jesus at Bethany" 61.
36. Malina, *New Testament World*, 182–83.
37. Resseguie, *Strange Gospel*, 86–87.
38. Malina, *New Testament World*, 84.

Temple, delineating spaces for transitioning from the profane to the marginal to the sacred. Mircea Eliade points to the symbolism of the "center" in religious practice and its role as a consecrated space where theophanies occur, a place where there is the possibility of the heavenly realm breaking into the earthly realm.[39] The tomb of Lazarus, then, becomes a consecrated place—a temporary but sacred center for the site of the miracle Jesus performs. As he performs the sanctification ritual, Jesus moves Lazarus from profane space to sacred space, and Lazarus passes from the world of death to the world of life. As Mary shares in the ritual, she also is "made holy," moving from the liminal, marginal space to the world of the sacred.

Raising Up: Jesus Reverses Sacrifice

Closely related to the idea of the sacred place is the notion of sacrifice, which means "to make (-fice) sacred or holy (sacri-), hence, to set apart to or for God, the nation, the family, or some other person."[40] One of the primary ways of interacting with God in the Temple was to celebrate or restore life, and the ritual of sacrifice was a means of providing restoration to individuals and communities after stepping outside the boundaries of the law.[41] Kristeva's understanding of ritual sacrifice is that it harnesses what would otherwise be random violence by channeling it toward a pre-chosen victim. The focus of violence on a particular subject "contains" potential chaos (associated with the semiotic realm) and establishes a sense of order and control (associated with the symbolic realm). With violence aimed at a specific victim, "the body, ultimately the semiotic maternal body, is sacrificed through the violence of the Symbolic."[42]

Here, however, what would be the sacrificial victim is *raised up* rather than sacrificed. We noted earlier the distinction Jesus makes between physical life and spiritual life: "Those who believe in me, even though they die, will live, and everyone who lives and believes in me will never die" (11:25–26). In the raising of Lazarus, Jesus restores physical life to the dead man and, at the same time, he restores spiritual life to Mary. She is introduced to a new life through Jesus who, like the maternal agency in the life of the developing subject has a primary role for bringing "into being the

39. Eliade, *Patterns in Comparative Religion*, 373.
40. Malina, *New Testament World*, 163.
41. Ibid., 185–86.
42. Oliver, *Reading Kristeva*, 40–41.

holiness ... of their babies' soul or spirit through oneness" with them.[43] Through this miracle, Mary also is "raised up," introduced to the fullness of life that is possible for her. Through purifying, sanctifying, and reversing sacrifice, Jesus restores Mary to right relationship with God.[44]

In-Breaking of another World

As we have seen, prior to the miracle, Mary stands in a liminal place between two worlds—the world she has known and the world she is about to discover. Like the child on the threshold of subjectivity and language, at the raising of Lazarus, Mary also witnesses the in-breaking of another world. In her journey as a developing subject, she has observed Jesus' love for the Father, and she has envisioned God the Father as an imaginary loving presence who can support and nurture her. Now, for the first time, she experiences God first-hand—not the imaginary vision she has formed through witnessing Jesus' love for the Father, not the transcendent and distant God of her tradition—but an immanent God present in the here and now.

At the beginning of this scene, Jesus also stands at the boundary of two worlds—the earthly realm and the heavenly realm and, as he calls forth Lazarus from the tomb, the two worlds come together. When Jesus performs the miracle in the view of all onlookers, he brings together "the world below" and "the world above" into one reality.

Until she witnesses the miracle, Mary's experience of the divine has been limited to pure signifiers—the name of God, Jesus' discourse about his relationship with the Father, and what she has learned of God from Scripture or tradition. This is equivalent to the "Name of the Father," Lacan's term for the prohibiting function of the father/law (*nom-du-père* or "Law of the Father," playing on the similar-sounding French words for name, *nom*, and no, *non!*).[45] Now, through witnessing the miracle of Lazarus being raised—a symbolic expression of the transcendent God being immanently present—Mary has a direct encounter with God the Father. By "making

---

43. Sayers, *Divine Therapy*, 228.

44. Jesus' actions of purifying, sanctifying, and reversing sacrifice are reminiscent of the three stages of divine initiative Brodie identifies in John's gospel: cleansing, purifying, and sanctifying. Since my analysis of Jesus' actions in the raising of Lazarus are based on Kristeva's theory of abjection and understanding of defilement/purification in the Judeo-Christian tradition, any similarity to Brodie's model is coincidental. See Chapter 1 for a description of Brodie's three stages.

45. Oliver, *Reading Kristeva*, 28, 46–47.

the *doxa* visible, by revealing the name,"[46] Jesus offers Mary a tangible experience of something previously only imagined.

Jesus' Revelation of God

As the scene opens, textual clues signal a shift in the way Jesus appears, and we can assume that, at the level of the story, Mary registers this difference and knows that something significant is about to occur. In the previous scene with Mary and the Judeans, we will recall that Jesus is described as "greatly disturbed in spirit and deeply moved" (ἐνεβριμήσατο τῷ πνεύματι καὶ ἐτάραξεν ἑαυτόν; 11:33b) but there, he is reflective, dwelling apart from the group, his only comment a simple question, "Where have you laid him?" (11:34). Brodie sees in this instance a self-emptying of Jesus that is heightened when he is invited to "come and see" (11:34)—an ironic twist because this is his usual command to others. In his self-giving, Jesus is "emptied of his sovereign status and knowledge."[47]

Now, when Jesus arrives at the tomb, he is described again as "greatly disturbed" (Ἰησοῦς οὖν πάλιν ἐμβριμώμενος; 11:38), yet this time he is very much in control, issuing a series of commands: "Take away the stone," (11:39); "Lazarus, come out!" (11:43); and "Unbind him, and let him go" (11:44). Spoken with authority, Jesus' commands show that it is God's power within him that enables him to bestow life.[48] These actions absolutely evoke God the Creator, and Jesus displays a "creator-like" authority. This is the fulfillment of his earlier promise that anyone who hears "the voice of the Son of God," even those already dead, will have eternal life.[49] Some scholars translate the word ἐμβριμάομαι in the sense of strength, as in "to strengthen oneself"; this is suggested by the noun form βριμή, which means "anger," "weight," or "power."[50] This translation is suggestive of a "breakthrough of spiritual power,"[51] indicating that Jesus is empowered by God immediately prior to the miracle. Even the name of the deceased signals God's direct

---

46. Counet, *John*, 310–11.
47. Brodie, *John*, 396.
48. Lee, *Symbolic Narratives*, 212–13.
49. Brodie, *John*, 396–97.
50. Danker, *Greek-English Lexicon*, 322.
51. Story, "Mental Attitude of Jesus at Bethany," 60–61.

participation in this scene: "Lazarus" is a Hellenized and shortened version of the Semitic "El-azar," which means "God helps."[52]

The Impact of the Revelation

The miracle Jesus performs in the raising of Lazarus is not just a "sign" to bring people to belief, but more importantly, it is the revelation of God's immanent presence in the world; we can imagine that Mary experiences this event as an in-breaking of divine power into her reality. Given that Jesus does nothing without the Father, the raising of Lazarus constitutes a miraculous irruption of the divine into the life of Mary and the others: "the raising to life of one who has died is nothing less than a manifestation of the glory of God."[53]

Although Lazarus is the direct recipient of the miracle, several others also benefit from it. Marianne Meye Thompson points out that characters who demonstrate faith in John's gospel—such as Martha and the other disciples—often are *not* the ones "who are the recipients of the healing or life embodied in Jesus' signs."[54] Sometimes, as in the case of the man at the pool (5:2–9), the character has no faith, yet is the one to receive healing. Thompson counters conventional wisdom about John's gospel that it is faith that brings about healing and life; she argues that the whole point of the Lazarus story is to illustrate that humans have no power to effect resurrection or new life. She argues persuasively that faith is not about what the believer does, that it is about something God does: "*God* must draw, and *God* must teach."[55]

It is clear that God's in-breaking in this scene has tremendous impact on several levels. First, when Jesus announced earlier that he was delaying his arrival in Bethany for a reason—in order to intensify the crisis of Lazarus' illness and death in such a way as to engender belief—we assume that he meant the disciples, since he said in their presence, "For your sake, I am glad I was not there, so that you may believe" (11:15). Yet there is no evidence that they respond in faith *during* or *after* the raising of Lazarus. We know from earlier scenes, however, that the disciples already have come to believe in Jesus: "Jesus did this, the first of his signs, in Cana of Galilee,

52. Brodie, *John*, 389.
53. Barrett, *John*, 335.
54. Thompson, "Raising of Lazarus," 242.
55. Ibid., 242.

and revealed his glory; and his disciples believed in him" (2:11); and "We have come to believe and know that you are the Holy One of God" (6:69). So, we can assume that the miraculous event *deepens existing belief* of the disciples present at the tomb, instilling in them a greater understanding of Jesus' oneness with God the Father. Second, because "Many of the Jews . . . who had come with Mary and had seen what Jesus did, believed in him" (11:45), it is clear that the miracle Jesus performs *fosters new faith* in selected observers. Additionally, we know that some of the Judeans present at the tomb testify to the chief priests, triggering their plans to put Jesus to death (11:46–53); for some, the miracle *evokes righteous anger*.[56] Finally, in Mary alone, the act of raising Lazarus *activates new birth* or birth from above. Interestingly, for all those present at the tomb, an encounter with Jesus, even one in which he performs a miracle of raising Lazarus from the tomb, is not enough to activate birth from above. It is only Mary for whom this event is transformative. As Jesus reveals the life-giving presence of God, it is Mary who is able to "perceive the divine radiance"[57] and be changed by it.

Kristeva borrows from Mikhail Bakhtin the concept of "the chronotope of the threshold," a literary strategy that describes a moment of change, crisis, or rupture—the places where epiphanies occur. Bakhtin and Kristeva connect this threshold with "the breaking point of a life," the moment that changes everything.[58] This is much more than an epistemological rupture or a change in cognition:

> There is an experience in life we call recognition. It is a kind of knowledge by which we apprehend meaning in a pattern of events or realize that the meaning we had once assigned to those events has been shattered . . . [This] experience of recognition is the central humanizing and revelatory experience, the immediate cause of psychological and spiritual change.[59]

This is the kind of recognition Mary experiences at the revelation of God in the miracle Jesus performs; it is a change at the deepest level of her being. In this *kairos* moment, we can imagine Mary suspended in the ineffable place of the semiotic—a space without form, language, or boundary, a space not unlike the plenitude of the *chora*.

56. Bennema, *Encountering Jesus*, 281–82.
57. Lee, *Symbolic Narratives*, 213.
58. Keltner, *Kristeva: Thresholds*, 7; Bakhtin, "Forms of Time," 248.
59. Culbertson, *Poetics of Revelation*, 9.

Signification and Meaning-Making

From Signs to Symbols

Ultimately, what Jesus does in the raising of Lazarus is move believers from the semiotic realm of signs-based faith to the symbolic realm of meaning. The relationship between signs (σημεῖον) and symbols in John's narrative is significant, especially since Jesus has repeatedly suggested that signs-based faith is not adequate: "Then Jesus said to him, 'Unless you see signs and wonders you will not believe'" (4:48; also 2:11, 18, 23; 3:2, 4:48, 54; 6:2, 14, 26, 30; 7:31; 9:16; 10:41; 11:47; 12:18, 37; 20:30).

Kristeva defines the word semiotic (σημεῖον) in the sense of its Greek meaning: "distinctive mark, trace, index, precursor sign, proof, engraved or written sign, imprint, figuration."[60] She acknowledges the similarities between the semiotic realm and signs in John's gospel, and she highlights several dimensions of a new "semiology" she believes the Fourth Evangelist creates. First, because the signs in John's gospel are in response to the physical and sensory needs of believers, Kristeva points out that John "adds a sensory layer to signs" analogous to the affective dimension found in semiotic expression. The miracle Jesus performs obviously responds to Lazarus' need for physical restoration. Second, instead of merely being fascinated to see the miracle itself, believers must receive the sign as a response to their need and next place their belief in Jesus as the one who provides for them. We do not know how Lazarus responds to this event, but we already have seen how it transforms the belief of all those present. Finally, Kristeva argues, because Jesus trusts in God the Father, believers should trust God as well; doing so requires the believer to open up to "a new interiority," which is a subjective understanding of the presence of the ultimate Giver.[61] This interior space allows the believer to make meaning of the event in the context of this understanding. For Kristeva, this progression mirrors "the subject's trajectory"; as a believer moves beyond merely witnessing the sign to physically receiving it and then to an interior, subjective space of trust, "the sensory foundation of John's semiology is transformed into an intensely symbolic dimension."[62] Although Mary's move toward meaning may be more profound and far-reaching than that of the others present at the tomb, as we witness the change in her that is evident later in the gospel

60. Kristeva, *Revolution in Poetic Language*, 25.
61. Kristeva, *New Maladies of the Soul*, 127–30.
62. Ibid., 130.

story, it is clear that part of her developing subjectivity involves opening to this new interiority and to a new understanding of the presence of God.

The distinction between signs and symbols in John is made clearly by Sandra Schneiders, who maintains that a sign stands for something *absent*, while a symbol is an expression of something *present*. She argues that a symbol is not a stand-in; rather, it is a "sensible expression" of something beyond, a revelation of something that transcends the world that cannot be apprehended directly. The purpose of a symbol in John's gospel, then, is to make the transcendent available to believers; in this way, "it is the locus of revelation (human or divine) and of participation in that which is revealed."[63] The miracle of raising Lazarus is not a sign, then; instead, it is a living symbol and the revelation of the very-present God. Through it, the divine presence is made available and immediate to believers.

John Painter's analysis of symbols in John's gospel explains further how symbols help observers experience the transcendent:

> . . . symbols are life-giving because they have the power to enhance the being of man, to create healthy (authentic) existence, by opening man's being to its transcendent source, to God. They enable man to see and therefore to choose the new way of being that has become possible through the revealer in whom God is present in life-giving power.[64]

By pointing to something beyond themselves, symbols also serve an important function in "the meaning that they open up" and the power they have to "help to make sense of human existence." By speaking to critical questions about the human situation—especially the question of "being or not being"—symbols provide a means for addressing the unanswerable questions at a human level and on a human scale.[65] It is quite reasonable to assume that Mary and the others present at the raising of Lazarus have heard Jesus' countless teachings about eternal life and everlasting life— "that whoever believes in him may have eternal life" (3:15); "This is indeed the will of my Father, that all who see the Son and believe in him may have eternal life . . ." (6:40); and "I came that they may have life, and have it abundantly" (10:10)—as well as his comments about passing from death to life—"Very truly, I tell you, anyone who hears my word and believes in him who sent me has eternal life, and does not come under judgment, but

63. Schneiders, "History and Symbolism," 372.
64. Painter, "John 9," 50.
65. Ibid., 48.

has passed from death to life" (5:24). Yet the significance and implications of Jesus' words have almost certainly remained a mystery to those who have heard him. Now, in witnessing the miracle of Lazarus being raised to life, Jesus' words become imbued with meaning. In seeing her brother resurrected, Mary now knows what it means for someone to pass from death to life. More importantly, the very act of witnessing the miracle and experiencing the in-breaking of God allows her to know first-hand what Jesus means when he speaks of eternal or everlasting life.

The creation of new meaning relates closely to the idea of Lazarus' tomb as a center or consecrated space. P. Joseph Cahill argues persuasively that "centering" not only is the site of "a breakthrough of the sacred," but also it is the site of new meaning, a new beginning, and a new reality. In his exploration of the symbolism of centering, Cahill makes a strong case for a *person* becoming a center:

> ... when a person is established as a center, it is primarily a subject that is at the center. This personal subject is a self-constituting being who has differentiated his consciousness to a high level; he has reached a stage of self-development of an elevated order, particularly in the realm of knowledge and love.[66]

Jesus is the one performing the miracle and, as a result, he is the *personal* center at the *physical* center of the tomb. But, given her central role in the narrative, it is not too great a leap to suggest that Mary, by extension, also becomes a center. And, as Cahill suggests, "When a person is established as a center there is a conscious, though implicit awareness, that what constitutes persons is their development as subjects and their progressive psychic differentiations."[67] Mary's presence *at* the center and *as* a center is a defining moment that launches her movement toward full subjectivity and a new life.

Conclusion

In Johannine terms, believers in this stage of coming to faith are said to "gain sight" or "accept Jesus" or "receive the revelation Jesus offers." This involves letting go of the past and turning away from the preoccupations of "the world below." In some cases, this happens upon seeing a sign, as in

---

66. Cahill, "Johannine *Logos* as Center," 62–63.
67. Ibid., 63.

the case with the man blind from birth in ch. 9, who responds to Jesus' sign by letting go of his past, releasing old ways of thinking, and renouncing old habits. He literally gains physical sight and spiritual sight, while the Pharisees continue to be "blind." Bultmann refers to this turning away from the world as the essence of faith:

> The demand for faith, therefore, is the demand that the world surrender the understanding it has had of itself hitherto—that it let the whole structure of its security... fall to ruins. Faith is a turning away from the world, an act of desecularization, the surrender of all seeming security and every pretense, the willingness to live by the strength of the invisible and uncontrollable.[68]

The experience of witnessing the raising of Lazarus is central to Mary's birth from above. This is the threshold of transformation for her, and the process of change she undergoes parallels that of the developing subject who moves beyond the semiotic *chora* into the realm of the symbolic. Just as the child moves toward the actual paternal figure, the broader social world, and the realm of language, Mary moves toward a new relationship with God the Father, an alternative reality, and the symbolic realm of signification/meaning.

Unlike the developing subject who moves into the symbolic realm of structured language, however, Mary's development is not about the primacy of the symbolic as logic, order, reason, and language. Here, the ultimate destination is authentic signification and meaning-making. Jesus leads Mary not to the symbolic system of rules, social order, and judgment—but to a new order of signification and meaning that he inaugurates. And, whereas traditional purification/sanctification rites involve separation, exclusion, Otherness, and a desire for heterogeneity, Jesus challenges this symbolic system. In the raising of Lazarus, Jesus converts profane space to sacred space, and his miracle serves to "reconcile and unite opposites."[69] Not only does he dissolve the boundary between the earthly realm and the heavenly realm, but also he overturns the distinctions between the profane and sacred, defilement and purity, signs and signification. Most importantly, he overturns death and restores life.

---

68. Bultmann, *Theology*, 2:75.
69. Cahill, "Johannine *Logos* as Center," 56.

4

A Radically Different Life

JOHN 12:1–8

Introduction

Just as Kristeva envisions the human person as a subject always in process, so she considers the meaning produced by that subject as dynamic rather than static. Speaking and writing are not reducible to a single, invariable sign-system, but instead comprise a signifying *process*. And because the speaking subject is a divided subject whose conscious and unconscious impulses find their way into language, Kristeva seeks to identify in any discourse the "semiotic disposition," the expression of the speaking subject's underlying drives, social constraints, or other influences. Out of this understanding of how meaning is produced, Kristeva proposes a way of reading texts—"semanalysis"—an approach that differentiates between the symbolic and the semiotic, attending not only to what the text signifies at the symbolic level, but also to the semiotic level of meaning embedded in it.[1] Kristeva acknowledges that biblical texts especially may lend themselves to this kind of analysis, precisely because reading a religious text strictly from the perspective of logic and rationality ignores the fact that "it conceals something that cannot be analyzed."[2] This reading strategy—of attending to the semiotic elements of the text—is particularly appropriate for John's gospel, given that the evangelist's writing style is far from linear

1. Kristeva, "System and the Speaking Subject," 28–29.
2. Kristeva, *New Maladies of the Soul*, 115.

and logical and features elements that are evocative rather than definitive. I employ this strategy in interpreting the anointing scene in order to reveal underlying themes that may not be apparent at the surface level of the text.

I also call upon another process closely related to semanalysis: Kristeva's understanding of transposition, "the signifying process' ability to pass from one sign-system to another . . ."[3] Through the process of transposition, a speaking subject takes a thetic position but, at the same time, complicates that position by introducing a *second* position. A new sign-system is introduced through the very language of the original sign-system: "this 'second truth' reproduces the path which was cleared by the first truth . . . in order to posit itself."[4] Transposition "alters the positions of enunciation and denotation, the positions from which the subject speaks as well as what it speaks about . . . [it] points to a shifting subject position, a subject in transformation, a 'subject-in-process/on trial.'"[5]

In reading the anointing text, I pay attention to evidence of transposition from one sign-system to another. Although my aim is not to suggest what the evangelist intended, it is possible to discover beneath the first, commonly accepted, truth of this text a "second truth." Most scholars agree that every detail in the Fourth Gospel has been selected to persuade readers that Jesus is the Christ and Son of God—as stated clearly in this verse: "But these are written so that you may come to believe that Jesus is the Messiah, the Son of God, and that through believing you may have life in his name" (20:31). John's gospel is seen as a unified narrative with Jesus at its center, a narrative whose primary unifying theme is Christology. From this perspective, every aspect of the narrative is oriented toward reinforcing Jesus' identity. Even character development is understood as being in the service of this goal—to convey to the reader that Jesus is the Christ: "Throughout the Fourth Gospel . . . characters act as foils—this is to say, they speak and behave in such a way that our understanding of who Jesus really is is enhanced."[6] While it is clear that Mary of Bethany in the anointing story plays a role in illuminating who Jesus is, my analysis explores the additional sign-system transposed over the original, and it reveals a second truth beneath the first—a truth about Mary.

---

3. Kristeva, *Revolution in Poetic Language*, 60.
4. Ibid.
5. Oliver, *Reading Kristeva*, 93.
6. Stibbe, *John as Storyteller*, 17, 25.

Chapter 12 begins by telling us that Mary and Martha are at a dinner given for Jesus in Bethany six days before the Passover. Also present is their brother Lazarus, but there are other guests as well, including Judas the Iscariot. Martha serves, and her brother Lazarus is one of those at the table with Jesus. The mention of Lazarus' presence at the dinner suggests that it may be a celebration of Jesus' raising him from the dead earlier in the story. After the scene is set, Mary takes the costly perfume made of pure nard, anoints Jesus' feet, wipes them with her hair, and the house is filled with the fragrance of the perfume. Judas speaks up, asking why the oil was not sold and the money given to the poor, but the narrator tells us that Judas is the disciple who would betray Jesus, that he cares nothing for the poor, and is a thief who keeps the common purse. Jesus responds to Judas by telling him to leave Mary alone, that she brought the oil for the day of his burial. His final statement is enigmatic "You always have the poor with you, but you do not always have me" (12:8).

The New Subject

By comparing the silent and grieving Mary we meet in the earlier verses of ch. 11 with the Mary we see in ch. 12—the one who anoints Jesus' feet in a gesture of abundant love—it is clear that she experiences a transformation between these two scenes. The anointing is narrated in just eight verses, but they are enough to reveal Mary's position as a new subject—a woman who has become herself.

A New Identity as a Child of God

Mary's movement toward a new identity follows the same trajectory of the new subject in Kristeva's construct. Initially, Mary's identity is shaped by her environment and by her close relationship with Jesus—just as the pre-subject infant's emerging identity is that of oneness with the maternal figure and the environment of the *chora*. Before witnessing the miracle of raising Lazarus and experiencing the profound change it evokes in her, Mary's self-understanding is determined by her family of origin, kinship group, and social world; she sees herself as a member of the Jewish community and a faithful follower of Jesus. Yet, at the same time, she must be aware that because she is a woman, she is not an official disciple, and her role is limited to supportive and secondary. In terms of her external image, we can assume that Mary is perceived by those around her as meek and withdrawn, and her leadership potential is not recognized.

Upon her brother's death, we can imagine that Mary's identity is "unsettled," that she experiences "those intermediate states' or 'non-states' that exceed distinctions like subject and object, inside and outside, where the subject finds her/himself 'alone, singular, untouchable, unsociable, discredited."[7] Given Kristeva's claim that abjection is an experience of being an outcast or stranger, at this point, Mary is temporarily "in exile" due to her experience of abjection and separation.

Ultimately, like the child who moves toward the realm of language and subjectivity, for Mary, it is exposure to a Third, an Other, that conditions her for developing an identity of her own. Recall that, in the process of separating from the mother, the pre-subject begins to identify with the imaginary father, a stage Kristeva calls "primary identification." The importance of this lies in the fact that the Other becomes a stand-in for the subject herself, so that identifying with this Third prepares the child to eventually accept herself as an object of love. Difference is a crucial element of identity: "The Third, then, is a necessary function for the subject's entrance into a disposition that conditions subjectivity and the life of signs."[8] We can imagine Mary's self-identity changing as she encounters the in-breaking of God into her reality, the Third who introduces her not only to difference and otherness but also to a new identity and a new understanding of herself.

In accepting the revelation of Jesus, in fact, Mary receives the power to become a child of God. She has been introduced to an intimate relationship with God, and she now has a new existence as part of the divine family and, along with a new family of origin, a new identity. She has been reborn "of God" (ἐκ θεοῦ; 1:13), and will have "a continuing existence within God's family as a child within that family."[9]

In John, the term ἐξουσία ("power" or "might";[10] 1:12; 5:27; 10:18; 17:2; 19:10–11) is used to convey the believer's right to be a child of God and, therefore, to participate in the divine life. But, because the word always is linked to the concept of life, it also suggests the ideas of power and ability.[11] As Mary claims her "right" to be a child of God, she also discovers

---

7. Keltner, *Kristeva: Thresholds*, 72.
8. Kristeva, *Tales of Love*, 26; Keltner, *Kristeva: Thresholds*, 51–52.
9. Van der Watt, *Family of the King*, 178–79; Vellanickal, *Divine Sonship*, 151.
10. Danker, *Greek-English Lexicon*, 352–53.
11. Van der Watt, *Family of the King*, 185–86; Vellanickal, *Divine Sonship*, 149–51.

her power as an independent self, much like Kristeva's new subject who assumes and tries out her emerging autonomy as an individual being. In addition, directly after the raising of Lazarus, we hear Caiaphas refer to Jesus gathering "into one the dispersed children of God" (11:52), and this is the first reference to "children of God" outside of the Prologue.[12] Appearing as it does in this point in the story, the children-of-God designation affirms Mary's new status and identity as a "power-filled" child of God.

The Subject (-in-Process)

Mary's experience of the in-breaking of God has constituted her as a separate self: "the revelation of God involves a revelation of self," because it is impossible to become truly aware of the presence of God without simultaneously becoming aware of having lived without God in one's life.[13] The recognition Mary experiences when she sees her brother called forth from the tomb is just this kind of awareness—the awareness of another dimension within the ordinary, the awareness of God's abiding presence, the awareness of her deepest and most authentic self that was hidden to her. As God the Father is revealed to Mary, her own selfhood is revealed to her as well:

> John's Mary story is the story of a woman who becomes herself . . . she discovers how she can offer herself, *her* faith, *her* love . . . she has become herself and is doing something which no one else has done . . . she learns to be herself . . . she learns to live.[14]

We also see Mary aligned with Jesus in this scene, the first and only time this occurs in John. One clue can be found in a pattern Mark Stibbe identifies throughout John's gospel. The pattern is characterized by an individual bringing a concern to Jesus, whose immediate response appears to be dismissive or negative, followed by a positive action or comment that resolves the concern.[15] The anointing story can be viewed through the lens of this pattern: Judas brings to Jesus his concern that the spikenard used by Mary could have been sold to help the poor. Jesus responds at first by saying, "leave her," then clarifies his response further by indicating that Mary's actions are for the sake of his burial preparation. In this instance, however,

12. Coloe, *Dwelling in the Household of God*, 96.
13. Brodie, *John*, 222–23.
14. Moltmann-Wendel, *Women around Jesus*, 57.
15. Stibbe, *John as Storyteller*, 21.

Mary is the one who initiates the controversial action that raises a concern, and this is a significant difference from other situations in which Jesus responds to problems or concerns. The way the pattern is reconfigured in the anointing story suggests that Mary is aligned with Jesus, rather than with Judas or the other disciples. Through this lens, we see Mary elevated in importance and portrayed as an ally, a disciple uniquely "partnered" with Jesus. She is now the primary character and subject of this scene, the one who *performs* an action rather than the one the action is *performed upon*. Mary is the initiator who honors Jesus in a profoundly moving way, who instigates questioning on the part of Judas, and who is responsible, through her gesture, for having a significant impact on all the guests present.

As Mary continues to develop as a subject, we see evidence again of the phenomenon Kristeva refers to as "rejection" (or negativity), the process of the developing subject being propelled toward subjectivity by moving back and forth in an oscillating motion between states of stasis and rejection.[16] We saw this early on in Mary's journey, as she alternated between separating from Jesus (rejection) and moving toward him (stasis). Now we see a similar tension in her anointing. On one hand, there is clear symbolic import in the familiar actions of foot washing, anointing, and unbound hair, representing stasis; as she anoints Jesus, she is following the community custom of anointing before burial. On the other hand, she differentiates herself with a subversive act of love; this is a semiotic expression from the deepest part of her that transgresses accepted norms of behavior. This element represents Kristeva's concept of rejection: "in its refusals, the semiotic breaks with received meanings."[17] As we will see, it is the combination of the symbolic and the semiotic that imbue Mary's actions with meaning and life and power.

Touching the Sublime

It is in this scene where we find Kristeva's theory of transposition operating. As we will see, the rhetoric, word selection, and sensory imagery in this text collectively convey a sense of grandeur and the sublime; and they all point to a specific truth about Jesus. At the same time, however, the language points to a second truth about Mary.

16. Kristeva, *Revolution in Poetic Language*, 70, 81, 172; Oliver, *Reading Kristeva*, 10–11, 19–22, 41–47.

17. Keltner, *Kristeva: Thresholds*, 29.

108   LOVE, LOSS, AND ABJECTION

A rhetorical analysis of this passage reveals what C. Clifton Black calls a "rhetoric of grandeur." Black likens the evangelist's style to that of Demetrius (first century BCE), particularly his tendency toward grandeur or magnificence—which can show up in unusual word arrangement, word selection, or subject matter. Three other rhetorical styles, commonly employed by Cicero (first century BCE) are the *plain* (used to give information), the *middle*, and the *grand* (which has the power to plant new ideas and transform the old). The Fourth Evangelist's discourse most closely approximates the grand style, which has the power to produce a sense of ecstasy (rather than persuade the hearer)—a combination of wonder and astonishment and a sense of the sublime. This style of grandeur or amplification produces what some call "abundant abundance," both powerful feelings and religious wonderment.[18] In the anointing text, we see two different types of rhetorical devices used by John to enhance the force of his message: language of the sublime and sensory imagery.

Language of the Sublime

Black claims that some words carry more gravity and consequently have more powerful impact on the listener, conveying a sense of "heft, fullness, and sonority."[19] Almost every word in the key verse in the anointing text (12:3) falls into this category.

- λίτραν ("pound"), a word used only in John, enhances the gospel's tendency toward amplification or rhetorical grandeur. Enhanced or amplified details such as this one produce a sense of ecstasy or a hint of the sublime.[20]
- μύρου is translated as "ointment" or "perfume," and it generally carries the connotation of being strongly aromatic.[21]
- νάρδου is a word for "an aromatic plant from which oil of nard is derived, (spike)nard,"[22] and it calls to mind a sense of nature, herbs, blooms, aroma.

18. Black, "The Words That You Gave to Me," 220–23.
19. Ibid., 227.
20. Ibid., 224.
21. Danker, *Greek-English Lexicon*, 661.
22. Ibid., 666.

- πιστικῆς is generally translated as "pure" or "genuine," although it literally means "faithful" or "trustworthy." It is the adjective form of πιστικός (*pistikos, "pertaining to belief"*), and it appears only two times in the New Testament (here and in the corresponding story in Mark's Gospel, Mark 14:3).[23] The use of the word in conjunction with νάρδου ("spikenard") is superfluous, meant to emphasize the sensory element of smell, since nard is highly aromatic.[24]

- πολυτίμου, usually translated as "expensive" or "valuable," is a word that suggests great value or great worth. Apart from the anointing story in John and in Matthew, this word appears only two times in the New Testament, and both times in relation to genuineness of faith or belief (Matt 13:46; 1 Pet 1:7).[25]

- ἤλειψεν means "to anoint by applying a liquid such as oil or perfume";[26] anointing is used for ritual, festival, or health reasons.

- ἐπληρώθη is a word meaning "to make full" or "to fill with"; other connotations associated with this word are "to fulfill" or "to bring to completion."[27]

- ὀσμῆς can be translated as "fragrance," and it also is reminiscent of "the quality of something that stimulates the sense of smell" or "the quality of something that affects the mind."[28]

All of these words have the impact and sonority to which Black refers and collectively convey a sense of ecstasy, the sublime, grandeur, value, extravagance, faithfulness, abundance, genuineness, fullness, and sensual experience. Black argues that this language portrays Jesus in terms of the sublime yet, because these words all appear in the single verse describing Mary's actions, they are more closely associated with her than with Jesus. What the text is telling us is that Mary carries these qualities herself or engenders them in the drama being enacted.

---

23. Ibid., 818.
24. Kurek-Chomycz, "Fragrance of Her Perfume," 337.
25. Danker, *Greek-English Lexicon*, 850.
26. Ibid., 41.
27. Ibid., 829.
28. Ibid., 728.

Sensory Imagery

John's account of the anointing has a heightened emphasis on the sensory elements, especially touch and smell. The author of John is aware of the symbolism of fragrance, and he uses a variety of senses in the narrative to emphasize Jesus' appreciation for "the sensory delights characteristic of earthly life, even as taking them to be signs of another reality."[29] But Mary's association with the fragrance also imbues *her* with the qualities of sensory richness and perception. At the same time that she is absolutely present in the moment, there is the suggestion of a deeper reality she experiences and wants to share with others at the gathering.

For Black, the gospel's rhetorical style is inevitable: the language of the Johannine Jesus must depart from the rhetoric used by the Jesus presented in the other gospels because "a metahistorical Christology requires for its expression a metahistorical rhetoric."[30] He contends that the rhetorical style of John's gospel is directly reflective of the author's Christology, the depiction of Jesus as the divine Son of God, the perfect revelation of God: "Jesus *speaks* as Jesus *is*."[31] The rhetorical style, then, reflects the divinity of Jesus. At the same time, all of the language and imagery in the anointing text refer to physical, sensory, and embodied experiences—also reflecting Jesus' humanity. The same is true for Mary as well; she is closely associated with the very human, sensual, and embodied elements of this scene, yet the language and imagery of grandeur point clearly to her experience of the sublime, her participation in the life of the Divine.

Mary's New Humanity

The Fourth Evangelist uses comparison and contrast to emphasize important theological motifs, one of which is gender pairs—characters presented in corresponding twosomes immediately following one another. In John, gender pairs "demonstrate that the new family of disciples established by the Johannine Jesus is decidedly and equally inclusive of women and men."[32] The anointing story is an example of such a gender pairing. In contrast to Mary's authentic love and faith and her prophetic vision, Judas sees only

---

29. Kurek-Chomycz, "Fragrance of Her Perfume," 336, 340.
30. Black, "The Words That You Gave to Me," 228.
31. Ibid., 229.
32. Beirne, *Women and Men in the Fourth Gospel*, 17–22, 25–26.

at a very superficial level; not only does he not see the spiritual meaning of Mary's actions, but he himself exhibits utter falsehood and insincerity, criticizing Mary's actions as he plans to betray Jesus.[33]

Here, we have two sign-systems: the first pointing to Judas' betrayal of Jesus and the other revealing a second truth about Mary. Through the portrayal of Mary juxtaposed with Judas, the evangelist communicates an ongoing tension between genuineness and falsehood; worth and worthlessness; self-giving and taking; fullness and emptiness; faithfulness and betrayal; knowing and ignorance; being and doing; sight and blindness; sensory awareness and dullness, inclusion and exclusion; living and dying. In her loving presence, Mary embodies all of the positive qualities, which also are the qualities of being a different kind of disciple and a different kind of human being.

Mary's Rebirth into Eternal Life

Jesus' actions in the raising of Lazarus usher in a new reality in the midst of the present reality—and this affects those who have died already ("Those who believe in me, even though they die, will live"; 11:25) *and* those still living ("and everyone who lives and believes in me will never die"; 11:26). Recall that, before witnessing the raising of her brother, Mary's sister Martha appears to believe in a traditional "end-time" resurrection. After the miracle, she may see that death is not a dead-end after all, that Jesus raises the dead to life even *prior* to the end time.[34] But, for Martha and the other onlookers, the focus is on physical restoration of the body. They fail to understand that the eternal life Jesus offers is so much more.

Similarly, prior to witnessing her brother being raised, Mary thinks only of this current existence, and her expectation that Jesus' presence is enough to prevent her brother's life from ending. Initially, she does not understand the deeper meaning in Jesus' words about eternal life—that it is not a future reality that comes after physical death or at the time of the end-time resurrection but a spiritual aliveness available to believers in the here and now. Jesus' earlier comments to Martha about eternal life (11:25–26) affirm the present reality, especially when read in conjunction with 5:21: "Indeed, just as the Father raises the dead and gives them life, so also the Son gives life to whomsoever he wishes" (5:21). The use of the present tense

---

33. Resseguie, *Strange Gospel*, 165.
34. Coloe, *Dwelling in the Household of God*, 89–90, 95.

for the verbs in this verse (ἐγείρει / "raises"; ζῳοποιεῖ / "gives life") highlights the fact that the raising and giving of life—by the Father and the Son—takes place in the present, not in some far-off future reality.[35] It refers not to the restoration of physical death or to the end-time resurrection, "but to those who are spiritually dead in the present because they have not heard of or have rejected the word of Jesus."[36]

Now Mary has discovered what Jesus' words of eternal life mean. She knows that he speaks of two kinds of life—physical life (ψυχή) and spiritual life (ζωή). This spiritual life is eternal because, for those who receive it, physical death becomes inconsequential; "life before death and life after death are all simply the same life."[37] Mary knows now that Jesus does not refer to an extension of natural life but instead to a life that is different in quality and character—a completely new existence that begins now, in the present, and will continue forever, "a qualitatively different kind of life" and "the whole person divinely alive."[38]

Society/Social Order

Mary's "Intimate Revolt"

In Kristeva's understanding, the Symbolic order (or Social order) encompasses the realm of signification and social rules, the order of law as well as accepted cultural, political, and religious convention. But, within this Symbolic order are symbolic *and* semiotic elements of language—both of which we know are essential for discourse to be meaningful. We already have seen how the semiotic element of language, for Kristeva, operates subversively in its tendency to disturb the logic and reason of socially-acceptable symbolic expression. So, while the symbolic element of discourse is what makes it possible for a speaker to take a position or make a judgment, the semiotic element is what works *against* that very position or judgment to create the momentum that keeps society moving forward. It is the dialectical tension between these two elements that is essential for new possibilities to emerge.

---

35. Schnackenburg, *John*, 2:106, 111.

36. Coloe, *Dwelling in the Household of God*, 97–98.

37. Clark-Soles, "I Will Raise [Whom?] Up," 42–43.

38. Schneiders, "Resurrection (of the Body) in the Fourth Gospel," 170–71; Clark-Soles, "I Will Raise [Whom?] Up," 49–50.

In the anointing scene, on one level, we see Mary operating within the accepted Social order of her society—the realm of cultural, kinship, and religious expectations. Yet, on another level, she disrupts the accepted order by transgressing boundaries. Her actions illustrate Kristeva's contention that "the Symbolic order is not just the order of Law . . . it is also the order of resistance to Law."[39] The deeper dimension that Mary is now able to perceive constitutes a new Social order—one that has emerged out of her own willingness to challenge the norms of the accepted Social order. Kristeva advocates for this kind of revolt—a word she interprets here not in the sense of political revolution but in the sense of "return," "displacement," or "anamnesis."[40] Based on this understanding, she sees revolt as crucial for an individual's freedom and happiness and for a society's justice and well-being. It is through this "intimate revolt" that an individual displaces authority within herself, is able to make meaning her own, and becomes assimilated into the Social order. And it is through this kind of transgression or displacement of authority that a society can open to new possibilities for creation, meaning, and human life.[41]

Jesus' Love Commandment

Kristeva suggests that the uniqueness of a mother lies precisely in her experience of loving someone who was once a part of her but is now a separate individual—an Other within. Out of this experience, Kristeva claims, mothers model how to "have a relationship with someone who is neither strictly self nor other."[42] Kristeva sees this as an ethical kind of love, a model for all subjective relations, all healthy societies.

As the maternal figure in Mary's developing subjectivity, Jesus models this kind of ethical, self-giving love. Not only does he demonstrate this love himself, but also he asks the same of his disciples: "I give you a new commandment, that you love one another. Just as I have loved you, you also should love one another" (13:34; also 14:15, 21; 15:10, 12, 14, 17). Brown points out the unusual idea of love as an order or command. But the love Jesus models is not a requirement for being in the community; rather, it is

39. Oliver, *Reading Kristeva*. 10.
40. Pollock, "Dialogue with Julia Kristeva," 6.
41. Groden, Kreiswirth, and Szeman, *Contemporary Literary and Cultural Theory*, 279.
42. McAfee, *Kristeva*, 85.

what constitutes and marks the community as distinctive. The use of the word "command" (ἐντολή; 13:34) indicates that what Jesus proposes is a new covenant with those he has chosen—as a restoration or replacement of the original covenant between God and God's chosen people.[43]

The word ἐντολή, although translated as "commandment," also closely relates to the word τέλος, which suggests the "fulfillment or completion" or "the goal toward which a movement is being directed."[44] This more nuanced understanding of the word indicates that the commandment Jesus speaks of is an internal force that prompts believers toward a desired end, toward completion or wholeness. It is in this sense that Mary embraces the love Jesus models.

Earlier we saw how Jesus emptied himself prior to the raising of Lazarus in preparation for being filled with the power and presence and authority of God. Mary's outpouring of love in the anointing scene evokes a similar self-emptying. The text tells us simply that "Mary took a pound of costly perfume made of pure nard, anointed Jesus' feet, and wiped them with her hair" (ἡ οὖν Μαριὰμ λαβοῦσα λίτραν μύρου νάρδου πιστικῆς πολυτίμου ἤλειψεν τοὺς πόδας τοῦ Ἰησοῦ καὶ ἐξέμαξεν ταῖς θριξὶν αὐτῆς τοὺς πόδας αὐτοῦ; 12:3). Yet the verb λαμβάνω also can be translated as "take hold of," "apprehend," or "take up," and the verb ἀλείφω is sometimes translated as "pour."[45]

So, on one level, Mary's anointing is clearly evocative of Jesus' washing the disciples' feet in ch. 13, when he removes his robe before washing the disciples' feet, then puts his robe on again (13:4–5). On a deeper level, the action of "taking up" and "pouring out" also calls to mind the self-emptying nature of Jesus' love. Considering the alternative connotations of the words in the anointing verse, it is possible to envision Mary's actions as a form of kenosis similar to that of Jesus, especially his willingness to lay down his life for his friends.[46] As Mary exemplifies Jesus' love commandment, she demonstrates the kind of relationship "that binds the subject to the other through love and not law . . ."[47] She is now bound to Jesus through love rather than through the Law.

---

43. Brown, *John XIII–XXI*, 612–13.
44. Danker, *Greek-English Lexicon*, 340, 998–99.
45. Ibid., 583–85, 41.
46. Miller, "Mary (of Bethany)," 483–84.
47. Oliver, *Reading Kristeva*, 183.

Mary's Rebirth into the Kingdom of God

As the first disciple in John's gospel "to live out Jesus' love commandment,"[48] Mary will be instrumental in keeping the spirit of Jesus alive within the community: "as long as Christian love is in the world, the world is still encountering Jesus."[49] As she anoints Jesus in an outpouring of love, everyone present at the dinner is affected: "and the house was filled with the fragrance of the perfume" (ἡ δὲ οἰκία ἐπληρώθη ἐκ τῆς ὀσμῆς τοῦ μύρου; 12:3).

Philip F. Esler and Ronald A. Piper contend that οἰκία in this verse refers to the inside circle of Jesus followers. The word also relates closely to the "house" imagery prevalent in the following chapter—"In my Father's house there are many dwelling-places" (14:2), as well as to Jesus' discourse about "his own" (17:9–16). In the anointing scene, then, it is this specific group of believers who benefits from Mary's actions; "they obtain a kind of air/spirit-borne anointing themselves."[50] Yet other commentators claim that the fragrance of the perfume represents the love and *gnosis* of God spreading to the whole world.[51]

The Otherness of God

Mary's developing subjectivity supports the idea of a broader reach; there are hints that, because of her, the community is to include those outside of the immediate circle of Jesus followers. We know this because, in the process of developing subjectivity, it is the child's exposure to thirdness, exteriority, and otherness that prepare her to be in relationship with other people. As a witness to the raising of Lazarus, Mary has been exposed to the Otherness of God breaking into her reality. Her exposure to God as an Other has allowed her to individuate and has opened her to love and authentic connections with those around her, because love is "the experience of social binding or of community with another."[52] Like the developing subject who learns to love through primary identification with the loving imaginary father, Mary learns what authentic love is through her encounter

---

48. Levine, "John," 300.
49. Brown, *John XIII–XXI*, 612, 614.
50. Esler and Piper, *Lazarus, Mary and Martha*, 68.
51. Bultmann, *John*, 415.
52. Keltner, *Kristeva: Thresholds*, 105–6.

with God the Father. Through this revelation of the Divine, her relationship with God has changed, and she now has a renewed relationship with those around her as well; "such a result is inevitable; one cannot come closer to God without changing one's relationship . . . to everything in the world which tends to set itself in God's place."[53]

The Otherness of Jesus

In addition, Mary knows the Otherness of Jesus. He speaks of himself as a stranger, one who comes "from above" (3:31; 8:23), the one who is not of "this world" (17:14; 18:36), and his own do not receive him (1:11). But also, as the maternal agency in Mary's process of rebirth, he has been abjected by her but, as Kristeva reminds us, part of the abject always stays with us, remaining at the borders of consciousness.[54] Jesus, who exists in a mother-like relationship with Mary, is the one who has facilitated her separation from him and her movement toward a new subjectivity. Because he has made her who she has become, he is a part of what constitutes her, an Other within. As a subject-in-process, Mary will continue to call on this Other within to move her to new levels of subjectivity: "He is the Other whom we are constantly called to learn more about, and thereby learn more about ourselves as well."[55]

The Otherness Within

Finally, Mary has encountered Otherness in herself; out of her own experience of abjection, she knows what it means to be a stranger, an exile. In the process of abjecting Jesus, she experienced the rejection of herself as well; not able to return to the place she started from, she has become like a homeless person, a stray, an exile.[56]

Kristeva advocates for a love built on embracing this alterity, and she sees the mother's ability to love the Other within as a model for all ethical love. In the early stages of subjectivity, the maternal agency allows space for the subject to develop, thereby allowing her freedom to become an individual in her own right. In this way, both separation and connection are

---

53. Brodie, *John*, 433.
54. McAfee, *Julia Kristeva*, 49–50.
55. Henriksen, *Desire, Gift and Recognition*, 81.
56. Kristeva, *Powers of Horror*, 8.

components of meaningful relationships; Kristeva envisions a new kind of community in which connection and alterity are in tension to form meaningful relationships.[57] Mary is uniquely positioned to create a community like the one Kristeva describes, one based on both connection and difference, a community in which strangers are welcome. As Kristeva reminds us, it is "the marginalized [who] are in the unique position to offer a different approach to power and meaning."[58]

This new community is nothing less than the kingdom of God Jesus refers to when he says, "no one can see the kingdom of God without being born from above" (3:3). On one level, the kingdom of God evokes a realm in which God "rules," an earthly kingdom in which God leads his people. In John, however, the term appears so seldom and, when it does, suggests "the unseen reality of God,"[59] a concept interchangeable with eternal life. Yet many commentators argue persuasively that, in John, the kingdom of God is a social category referring to a new kind of community ushered in by God. This is a community in which believers are "born into fellowship with one another," living in "mutual love and solidarity" characterized by love of God and love of one another.[60] In this new Social order, Jesus' followers are called to live out their love for each other and to reorient their lives toward this end; it is not "a replacement for life in this world but . . . a new world *within* this world."[61] Not only is Mary reborn into this new world, but also she is instrumental in bringing it about.

Realm of the Symbolic

By the time Kristeva's developing subject enters the realm of symbolic language, she already has been producing meaning by way of semiotic expression; we saw this in Mary, especially in the early scene with Jesus (11: 28–32), in which she knelt at his feet and wept. But Kristeva is quick to point out that semiotic expression—although it is "pre-thetic" in the sense that it exists in the *chora* before the subject takes up a position that characterizes

---

57. Kristeva, *Strangers to Ourselves*, 80–81, 83; Guberman, *Julia Kristeva Interviews*, 41.
58. Keltner, *Kristeva: Thresholds*, 129.
59. Van der Watt, *Family of the King*, 175–77.
60. Gaventa, *From Darkness to Light*, 137–38, 143.
61. Nissen, *John*, 49–50.

the thetic break—cannot be understood as "prior" to the symbolic.[62] In fact, Kristeva continually insists on the dialectical tension between the two, and she characterizes the thetic not just as the realm of positions but as the threshold of "two heterogeneous realms: the semiotic and the symbolic" that "function synchronically within the signifying process of the subject himself."[63]

Because the semiotic is always a part of the realm of meaning, when the subject takes on symbolic language, the semiotic is not left behind. As we will see, in the anointing scene, Mary's actions have a distinct symbolic character but, at the same time, are imbued with an energy and power that can only come from the semiotic realm.

A New Language

Mary's actions in anointing Jesus are an example of what Kristeva would call "non-speech," an unvoiced form of communication that articulate underlying semiotic expressions. As we have seen, Kristeva views silence, tears, and other forms of non-verbal communication as expressions of the subject's deepest drives.[64] Yet clearly Mary's actions are not merely semiotic in that they have a great deal of symbolic meaning—the meaning is carried by the combination of the semiotic and symbolic elements.

In enacting the anointing, Mary demonstrates Kristeva's understanding of meaning production—that the semiotic and symbolic are critical for all discourse. In her view, it is the relation between the two that makes meaning possible: it "is constituted in the *dialectical tension* between the semiotic and the symbolic . . . a semiotic discharge of energy in the symbolic or . . . the giving of symbolic form and meaning to the semiotic."[65] Mary's act has meaning in her social-symbolic universe; for the onlookers in this scene, it signifies her anointing Jesus in preparation for his death and is an affirmative expression of meaning in the social world in which she lives. At the same time, it is an expression of a semiotic impulse—Mary's outpouring of love for Jesus and her desire to express this love regardless of the boundaries of social conventions she must cross in order to do so.

---

62. Oliver, *Reading Kristeva*, 28–31.
63. Kristeva, *Revolution in Poetic Language*, 29, 48; Oliver, *Reading Kristeva*, 31.
64. Oliver, *Reading Kristeva*, 174.
65. Keltner, *Kristeva: Thresholds*, 19, 22.

Mary as Symbol-Bearer

This scene clearly illustrates Schneiders' contention that symbols lead individuals into the unknown by making it possible for them to subjectively experience the mystery of the transcendent. A symbol does not impart objective information, nor can it be explained as representing one thing only; instead, it is by its nature only meaningful through spiritual imagination or intuition. As an individual becomes involved with the symbol and enters into its revelation, it becomes a transforming experience.[66]

Earlier, in the raising of Lazarus, we saw how Jesus mediated various symbols in order to reveal the transcendent God—the raising of Lazarus was a symbol of divine possibility and power, as was Jesus himself a symbol of the transcendent God's in-breaking presence. In the anointing scene, it is Mary's turn to be the bearer of symbols, symbols that also represent the transcendent. The symbols that are central in this scene are foot washing, anointing with oil, and unbound hair—all of which point to a reality deeper than the one taking place at the level of action.

Foot-washing

When Mary anoints Jesus' feet, it is in the context of a culture in which foot-washing was commonplace, although generally people did not wash or anoint the feet of others. The practice of foot-washing is documented in biblical and Greco-Roman sources; guests arriving at someone's home after a long journey would find a basin and water to use for washing their feet before the meal. Only a slave or servant would ever be expected to wash someone else's feet, and anyone volunteering to do so would be seen as that person's slave. Mary's actions are most commonly seen as an act of devotion to Jesus and, although her anointing is associated with serving another, it is not understood as an act of servitude.[67] Mary's anointing symbolizes and "models the kind of love that is to characterize Christian life,"[68]—and it is the kind of love and care that transcends ordinary social conventions. As we have seen, the foot washing also has greater implications for the community itself.

---

66. Schneiders, *Written That You May Believe*, 65–69.
67. Koester, *Symbolism in the Fourth Gospel*, 127–28.
68. Ibid., 134.

Anointing with Oil

The oil, made from an exotic, imported aromatic herb, is extremely expensive, suggesting the richness and extravagance of Mary's giving. On one level, it points to the significance of Jesus' being hailed the "King of Israel" by the crowds soon afterwards, although traditionally kings were anointed not on the feet, but on the head.[69] Some believe that the detail of anointing the feet in John's gospel, as opposed to anointing of the head in the Synoptics, relates specifically to the burial motif: the head of a living person is anointed, and the feet of a corpse are anointed in preparation for burial.[70] But the act of anointing has other connotations as well. In Isa 61:1, anointing is associated with the gift of the Spirit: "The spirit of the lord God is upon me, because the LORD has anointed me" (Isa 61:1), suggesting that Mary pours out the Spirit upon Jesus. Anointing also is associated with the gift of power: "God anoints Jesus with the power of the Holy Spirit at his baptism and the woman in our passage is portrayed as bestowing power upon Jesus."[71] At the same time, Mary *herself* is anointed: "For the effect of wiping Jesus' ointment-bearing feet with her hair is that her head has been anointed via the body of Jesus"[72]—suggesting that she, like Jesus, has been given the power of the Holy Spirit.

Unbound Hair

Traditional interpretations see Mary's hair as a detail that reinforces the self-effacing nature of her act. In the ancient world, the absence of well-kept hair is frequently seen as related to an absence of dignity and a degrading position.[73] Yet Charles H. Cosgrove points to several other potential meanings for the social symbolism of unbound hair in our story. According to Cosgrove, a woman's unbound hair could be an expression of "thankful veneration," "a gesture of humility and reverence," "a symbolic self-offering to the god," the desire to participate in a ritual "in a pure and natural state," a symbol of freedom or naturalness, a symbol of grieving or anticipatory grief in the face of danger, preparation for baptism, to "effect simplicity,

69. Ibid., 129–30.
70. Brown, *John I–XII*, 454.
71. Miller, "The Woman Who Anoints Jesus," 221–36.
72. Esler and Piper, *Lazarus, Mary and Martha*, 66.
73. Koester, *Symbolism in the Fourth Gospel*, 129.

lack of ostentation, naturalness," an ecstatic state, or "a state of extremity or liminality."[74] Many of these are relevant to Mary's unbound hair in this story; we can envision her as grateful, reverent, humble, pure, natural, free, ecstatic, and in a state of liminality.

In a scene that is traditionally understood to be about Jesus' impending death then, we can find another sign-system highlighting Mary's act of self-giving, one that emerges from her new subjectivity. It is Mary who mediates the transcendent for those gathered at the dinner, and her actions affect everyone present. Through anointing Jesus' feet, she demonstrates loving humility, vulnerability, and self-emptying. It is an act of self-giving love and reverence rather than one of servitude, debasement, or denigration. Mary has entered a reality beyond herself, one in which abundant love overflows from the depth of her being, and she makes present for others this deeper reality she inhabits, allowing them to experience it through her.

Mary's Sign Act

Mary Coloe highlights a liturgical background for Mary's anointing of Jesus: the *Habdalah* ceremony taking place at the conclusion of the Sabbath, a ceremony featuring a shared meal, aromatic spices, and an anointing. One of the primary purposes of the *Habdalah* ritual was to anoint objects, persons, or spaces with special spices in order to make them holy and set them apart for God's service—as God directs Moses to do with the tabernacle, altar, and Aaron in Exod 40:9–13.[75]

When Mary performs the anointing then, she replicates the actions of Moses in a ritual that onlookers would have recognized. First, following the tradition of the *Habdalah* in distinguishing between the sacred and profane, she marks the space as holy. Second, like the *Habdalah*, her actions signal a transition from ordinary to sacred time. And finally, like Moses in anointing the tabernacle, Mary marks Jesus as "the tabernacle[76] of God's presence."[77] Here, we see Mary performing a sign-act in the prophetic tradition just as Jesus did in the raising of Lazarus—a sanctification ritual to mark the movement of both space and time from the profane to the sacred *and* a ceremony to mark Jesus' manifestation as the tabernacle of God.

74. Cosgrove, "A Woman's Unbound Hair," 676–91.
75. Coloe, *Dwelling in the Household of God*, 114–15.
76. Conway, *Men and Women in the Fourth Gospel*, 151.
77. Coloe, *Dwelling in the Household of God*, 114–15, 119.

Some sources also suggest that the *Habdalah* was known for liturgically blessing the ending of Sabbath because it signaled the leave-taking of a "second soul" present with believers during the Sabbath: the "sweet-smelling spices symbolize the spiritual farewell 'feast' for the departing 'additional soul' which the Jew figuratively possesses on the Sabbath."[78] This connection is consistent with the view that Mary's anointing is a pre-figuring of Jesus' death; he is the departing "second soul" present with those at the dinner. Although Jesus' comment to Judas is puzzling—"Leave her alone. She bought it so that she might keep it for the day of my burial" (12:7)—it makes sense when considering that the word for "burial" (ἐνταφιασμός) also can be translated as "preparation for burial."[79] This interpretation suggests that Mary prophetically anticipates that Jesus' death is near and, in anointing him, prepares his body ahead of time.[80]

Out of all the disciples, Mary alone is aware of the certainty and the meaning of Jesus' imminent death. She has suffered the death of her brother, has witnessed him being miraculously raised to life again, and has experienced the in-breaking presence of the transcendent God. Now she understands that Jesus is going to die, and she knows it is the cost of him restoring her brother to life. She responds to Jesus' self-giving love with a self-giving response, "pouring, in the flow of the myrrh, her own self in love"[81] for him.

In the anointing, then, Mary performs a ritual of purification and sanctification and, in pouring out her love for and intimacy with Jesus, exemplifies union within the community of believers. The anointing mirrors Jesus' earlier actions in the raising of Lazarus, in which he purifies, sanctifies, and calls Mary and the others into relationship with God the Father. At the same time, the anointing prefigures Jesus' washing of the disciples' feet in the following chapter (13:1–12): "in the washing of their feet, Jesus will draw them into union with himself, purifying and transfiguring them in relationship with him."[82]

Whereas earlier, she abjected Lazarus' death and his corpse, now at the anointing, Mary accepts Jesus' impending death fully and does not turn away. Earlier she fell at Jesus' feet in sorrow and hopelessness, and now she

---

78. Millgram, *Jewish Worship*, 297; Coloe, *Dwelling in the Household of God*, 114–15.
79. Danker, *Greek-English Lexicon*, 339.
80. Miller, "Mary (of Bethany)," 480.
81. Ibid., 207.
82. Lee, *Flesh and Glory*, 208, 211.

places herself again at his feet—only this time in reverence, awe, and love. At a time when Mary stood in a liminal place on the threshold of a new reality, Jesus facilitated her movement from the profane to the sacred, from estrangement to relationship, and from spiritual death to spiritual life. In this scene, as Jesus stands in a liminal place and time, on the threshold of the ultimate boundary—death,[83] Mary is the one beside him, honoring this holy moment of transition.

Receiving Jesus as "the Word"

We have seen how Mary, before becoming a subject, had not yet received Jesus as "the Word." But Jesus, in the raising of Lazarus, demonstrated that he is "the revealer of God, the symbol for God in relation to the world, through whom God is known,"[84] Jesus as the Logos has made it possible for Mary to experience the in-breaking of God the Father into her world and, through this event, Mary has received Jesus as "the Word."

John Painter persuasively argues that, in John's gospel, responding to "the Word" of God is equivalent to the Genesis theme of being created in the image of God. Human beings, having failed to realize their potential as beings made in God's image, have the opportunity to overcome their failure by hearing "the Word" of God in Jesus, by accepting the revelation of God in Jesus. Painter expresses the potential in this way:

> Man should be a bearer of the revelation and, through the revealer, divine love is manifest in human life so that the disciples become extensions of the revealing event to the world (13.35) . . . symbols of the revelation. The possibility . . . is dependent on the perception of man, whether or not he sees the object pointing beyond itself, through the revealer, to God. . . The purpose . . . is to present man with the choice, for or against the revealer, for his present existence or for the new possibility opened up by the revealer.[85]

At one level of the text, the Lazarus miracle makes it clear that Jesus is the Logos, the revealer, but we can find hints at a deeper level that Mary also has become a bearer of the revelation. Because she alone sees beyond the "sign" to the tangible presence of God the Father and because she makes

---

83. Coloe, *Dwelling in the Household of God*, 122.
84. Painter, "John 9 and the Interpretation of the Fourth Gospel," 47–48.
85. Ibid., 51.

a choice for a new existence opened up to her by Jesus, Mary carries the revelation to others in the community of Jesus followers. She now becomes a symbol of the Logos herself, exemplifying a type of presence that characterizes being fully alive and fully human.[86]

In the anointing, Mary mirrors the symbolic and ritual practice Jesus enacted in the raising of Lazarus. First, as Jesus purified defilement in bringing death to life, Mary purifies Jesus in the washing of his feet. Second, Jesus' act of sanctification at Lazarus' tomb is reflected in Mary's anointing—pouring out of the Spirit on Jesus and making the space holy—and her marking his impending death with a ritual similar to the *Habdalah*. And, finally, just as Jesus in the raising of Lazarus resolves Mary's estrangement from herself, her community, and God—so too does Mary, in bearing the revelation to the others present at the meal, resolve the separation and mark the new community of Jesus. In her actions, Mary expresses herself from the depth of her new subjectivity; she brings together the community of disciples; and she expresses love, reverence, and gratitude to Jesus and to God the Father.

Mary's Rebirth into Abiding Unity and Divine Friendship

Mary exemplifies what Dorothy Lee describes in her theology of "abiding" in John's gospel: "an alternative vision of freedom, selfhood, and community."[87] Lee argues that the expression μένειν ἐν ("to abide in") appears in some form approximately forty times in the gospel—pointing to either a literal meaning of "to stay" or "to remain" or in a figurative sense of stillness and contemplation. This idea of abiding redefines discipleship away from achievement or outward orientation: "to be a disciple has more to do with being than acting."[88]

Essential to this abiding are an authentic knowledge of one's self, a deep awareness of one's personhood, and a strong identity. It is not a move toward individualism, however, in that authentic selfhood is precisely what facilitates authentic relationship with others. Abiding leads to mutuality in relationships, living "together in a community that works to overcome

86. Ibid., 67.

87. Lee, "Abiding in the Fourth Gospel," 77–78.

88. Ibid., 76. Lee's distinction between being and doing is not to be confused with the long tradition of seeing Mary as representing the contemplative life and Martha the active life. For Lee, abiding is not passivity or quietude; instead it is a powerful creative, fertile, and generative force.

alienation and isolation, individualism and hierarchy."[89] In Lee's construct, humans are not objects called by God to servitude or obedience; instead they are invited into friendship, subject-to-subject, finding their authentic selves in the process. Lee expresses the beauty and uniqueness of this "kinship" with God:

> The divine "I am" stands in personal relation to human becoming, so that human beings find in themselves a subjective "I am," a sense of selfhood that is itself the gift of an incarnate God. Abiding defines the divine-human relationship as one of immanence: subject-to-subject, face-to-face, I-Thou . . .[90]

Mary finds this sense of abiding, and we can see it in her silent, yet powerful presence, her impact on everyone gathered at the meal, and her participation in the divine life. Having experienced Jesus' self-giving love and the loving presence of God, she now is able to rest in an abiding, loving unity with both. Like Kristeva's subject who needs the presence and engagement of both a maternal and a paternal figure for wholeness and health, Mary reaches a place of love, wholeness, and intimacy with both Jesus and God.

Yet Mary's relationship with Jesus and God is no longer analogous to the relationship of a child to her mother and father. She has moved *beyond* the family model to a new kind of relationship the evangelist can only describe in terms of friendship. This friendship is based on the divine love underlying all of creation—a love that is evident in the incarnation itself and that overflows into the world. We see several dimensions of this love in John's gospel: 1) the love of God for creation, which is the foundation of the Father-Son relationship and is manifest in God's sending of the Son into the world; 2) the love Jesus has for the disciples, which is demonstrated in his life and death; 3) the love of the disciples for Jesus, which is in response to God's self-giving in Jesus; and 4) the love of the disciples for each other, which is to be the foundation of the community's life.[91] All of these relationships, which have their foundation in the love of the Father and the Son, are characterized by abiding friendship, which is "primarily a quality of the divine realm, an aspect of eternal life that in John's Gospel is offered to all human beings . . . as a heavenly quality, it expresses the intimacy and

---

89. Ibid., 75.
90. Ibid.
91. Lee, "Friendship, Love and Abiding," 57–59.

reciprocity that lie at the heart of the universe."[92] In her transformation, Mary is birthed into this abiding, divine friendship.

Mary's Journey of Rebirth

Most commentators identify the raising of Lazarus as the narrative center of John, the last miracle in the Book of Signs and the turning point that moves the story toward Jesus' death and resurrection. Many John scholars have identified compositional structures to demonstrate the passage's centrality to the larger gospel story.[93] I have identified a narrative structure in ch. 11 and 12 that reflect Mary of Bethany's developmental journey toward being fully human. The narrative arc of Mary's journey traces her movement in toward the narrative center and then out again:

A   Mary exists in a false security/union with Jesus
 B   Death enters her world; she abjects death and separates from Jesus
  C   Mary falls at Jesus' feet in sorrow and hopelessness
   D   Mary sees herself reflected in Jesus' weeping
    E   Jesus sanctifies, purifies, and resolves estrangement
     F   Jesus raises Lazarus; in-breaking of God into the world
    E' Mary sanctifies, purifies, and creates community
   D' Mary becomes aligned with Jesus
  C' Mary places herself at Jesus' feet in reverence, awe, and love
 B' Death will enter her world; she does not turn away but stands with Jesus
A' Mary abides in divine friendship and unity with Jesus and with God

Conclusion

In Johannine language, those who reach this final stage—having been born from above—know that Jesus is the one sent by God (17:7–8, 25), understand him to be the unique revelation of God, and receive God's words and truth through him (17:7–8). Believers also know the "truth" promised to

---

92. Lee, *Flesh and Glory*, 99.
93. See, for example, Lee, *Symbolic Narratives*, 188–226.

them (8:32), that God is the ultimate reality and the world's "reality" is a falsehood. If they are born from above, believers have rejected the world's falseness, allowed their actions to be directed by the truth, and centered their lives in Jesus. They also acknowledge their dependence on God as the source of all life, understand their reliance on Jesus, and recognize their responsibility to continue the work of Jesus in the world. Finally, they experience eternal life and share in the relationship Jesus has with God.

Mary's experience of birth from above expands our vision of the born-from-above believer. In her interactions with Jesus, she is transformed, both *inwardly* at the level of her being and *outwardly* in her response to others. Her transformation is not contingent on believing in Jesus, performing certain behaviors, or exhibiting obedience or submission. Instead, it involves her claiming full and authentic selfhood; showing recognition, solicitude, and care for others in her community; and being open and responsive to the revelation of God in Jesus. Mary's new identity (self), her new relationship with the community (Self and Other), and her new relationship with Jesus and God (self and God) are what characterize a born-from-above individual.

This reading of Mary's story also enhances our understanding of what it means to be fully human in John's gospel. Although Mary has been transformed, she will continue to know sorrow in her life; in fact, she alone knows of Jesus' impending death, and we can imagine the profound sorrow she will feel. But we also can envision her bearing the grief in a different way, not only because she lives in abiding unity with Jesus and God, but also because she has experienced eternal life and knows that nothing is ever lost to God. Mary models for us what it means to be fully human according to John—to hold the reality of human life in one hand while holding the joy of eternal life in the other.

5

The Journey of New Birth

Long before I started this project, I was interested in the relationship between new birth alluded to by the Johannine Jesus and the type of experience we would today call transformation—a process by which an individual's meaning system is substantially altered, resulting in profound changes in how he or she experiences and understands God, the self, relationships with others, and the world.[1] In my early readings of John, Mary of Bethany appeared to be the only one out of all the characters in John's gospel to undergo the kind of transformation that might be characterized as birth from above.

I wondered, too, whether the concept of rebirth in John's gospel might be more than a metaphor, whether it might describe a process analogous to the development of human selfhood occurring early in life. Mary's story has, in fact, proved to be an appropriate "case-study" for exploring this premise, in that her transformation over the course of the narrative closely parallels the progress of the developing subject in infancy—in the child's movement from the safety of the semiotic *chora* through the various processes that bring her to the threshold of language, initiate her into the Social order, and constitute her as an individual subject. Mary's journey follows a similar trajectory as she moves from the comfort of her very circumscribed world to an alternative reality—gaining empowered selfhood, a relationship of mutuality and solidarity with her community, and an abiding friendship with Jesus and God.

---

1. Paloutzian and Park, *Handbook of the Psychology of Religion and Spirituality*, 334–35, 338–39.

Using Kristeva's psychoanalytic theory as a hermeneutic has been extremely useful for defining birth from above in John, for understanding the process by which this transformation occurs, and for identifying the characteristics of a born-from-above individual. This interpretive approach has given me the freedom to explore the questions I raised earlier, to find in the biblical text possible responses to the life-altering concerns that are directly relevant to our contemporary lives and struggles.

Why does Mary behave so differently from her sister Martha?

By reading Mary's story intertextually with Kristeva's theories, we have been able to envision both sisters living in a safe, protected environment—the world of illusion John describes as walking in darkness, being spiritually blind, or living in "the world below." Yet, Mary emerges as someone in the earliest stages of a journey of rebirth. In sharp contrast to her sister Martha, who is complacent in her willingness to accept the meaning that has been given to her, overly attached to what she already knows to be true,[2] we have seen in Mary a humility and openness that leads her in new directions. In Martha, on the other hand, we witness an expectation of miraculous healing from Jesus that does not represent true belief: ". . . it is a misunderstanding if 'faith' expects from Jesus as miraculous liberation from physical distress."[3] Mary is the one whose faith is called into question as she alternates between hoping in Jesus and being disappointed by him—rejecting him at one moment yet being open, humble, and receptive at other moments. As I understand this narrative now, it is precisely this dialectic that sets up the possibility for a deeper, more genuine relationship of mutuality and love between Jesus and Mary.

Why does Jesus respond the way he does?

In Mary's journey toward rebirth, Jesus not only guides and supports her toward newly reconstituted selfhood but also enables her to experience an in-breaking of the Divine. In Johannine language, this is expressed as believing in Jesus, accepting Jesus as "the Word," receiving the revelation Jesus offers, or turning away from "the world below." Here, Mary's experience

---

2. Keltner, *Kristeva: Thresholds*, 36.
3. Bultmann, *John*, 207.

is set beside that of her brother Lazarus, who is raised from the dead and restored to physical life. As she witnesses the miracle, she too is "raised up" to a spiritual life, and she recognizes that everything she believed important prior to this moment pales in comparison to the in-breaking of God directly into her life: "all earthly goods are mere appearances in relation to the revelation."[4] This interpretation suggests that Jesus responds differently to each individual, and his role in Mary's story is to facilitate her journey toward new birth.

Why does Mary anoint Jesus' feet and what does it mean to her?

In the final phase of birth from above, Mary exists in a radically new life, one that emerges from the profound recognition she has in witnessing her brother raised to life. Here, the evangelist contrasts her with another disciple, Judas; her authenticity, integrity, and love are placed beside his betrayal, dishonesty and falsehood. At this stage, we see that Mary is (re)constituted as a subject, gains a new identity as a child of God, has a renewed relationship with her community, and participates in the divine life. In Johannine language, she has found eternal life, entered the kingdom of God, and abides in unity with Jesus and God. This is a new life within the present life:

> Birth from above gives the one who believes a totally new existence. Such a person still lives in this world in the flesh, but this way of existence is transcended by the birth from above. The same person lives within two levels of reality.[5]

What does it all mean to me?

This reading has allowed me to create new meaning out of Mary's story. First, I now see the experience of human loss and separation in a different light. One of the dimensions of Kristeva's theory that is especially relevant to this is what Kristeva calls "the subject in process" (*le sujet en procès*). Kristeva chooses this phrase to express the idea that the human being is always in a process of becoming, continuously shaped by relational influences, and never definitively "established" as a subject. But Kristeva's

---

4. Bultmann, *John*, 228.
5. Van der Watt, *Dynamics of Metaphor*, 174.

alternate interpretation of "the subject in process" as "the subject on trial" suggests a deeper level of engagement. In the dialectic tension that exists in the subject's signifying process, she is continuously alternating between the semiotic and symbolic elements of meaning, between rejection and stasis, and between maintaining the accepted order and transgressing the boundaries of that order. It is in this movement, this being-on-trial experience in which an individual reaches new levels of subjectivity.

In John, we encounter something similar in the word κρίσις—which occurs several times throughout the narrative (3:19; 5:22, 24, 27, 29, 30; 7:24; 8:16; 12:31; 16:8, 11), and is variously translated as "judgment," "condemnation," or "damnation,"[6] always in conjunction with divine judgment of sin, usually the sin of rejecting Jesus. Humanity is believed to be "on trial" for rejecting the revelation of Jesus, turning away from the gift of life and salvation offered by God. In the Nicodemus discourse, this is expressed as preferring darkness to light:

> And this is the judgment, that the light has come into the world, and people loved darkness rather than light because their deeds were evil (αὕτη δέ ἐστιν ἡ κρίσις ὅτι τὸ φῶς ἐλήλυθεν εἰς τὸν κόσμον καὶ ἠγάπησαν οἱ ἄνθρωποι μᾶλλον τὸ σκότος ἢ τὸ φῶς, ἦν γὰρ αὐτῶν πονηρὰ τὰ ἔργα; 3:19).

But the word *κρίσις* also is translated as "separation" or "sundering," a concept strikingly similar to Kristeva's understanding of abjection. Mary's journey, in fact, is a journey of the subject on trial; the pattern is clear in her deeper engagement in an encounter with death, in her relationship with Jesus, and in her experience of the in-breaking of God. It is the "approach-and-retreat" dialectic in her interactions with Jesus and God that moves Mary to a new level of subjectivity and faith. As *le sujet en procès*, Mary's "trial" is most apparent in her experience of separation and dispossession from the life and world she has known, and this interpretation illustrates the profound change she experiences as a result. Several implications emerge from this reading.

First, this analysis of Mary suggests that the trial believers encounter in John is an experience of profound separation and dispossession, and that this becomes the site of new creation. Turning away from "this world," kenosis, abjection, trial, or κρίσις—these are different ways of understanding the process of making space for a new self and a new reality. In Mary's

---

6. Danker, *Greek-English Lexicon*, 569.

story, John gives us a story of rebirth based on the "fundamental experience of human existence as one of dispossession."[7] Mary's journey mirrors the process of developing subjectivity, and it mirrors Jesus' journey to the cross. In her, we see that rebirth emerges out of an experience of profound separation from the one who gives us life—but it is a separation that leads to the birth of a reconstituted self, allowing for a deeper understanding of those once considered Other, and to a more trusting and authentic relationship with the Divine.

Second, this interpretation demonstrates that Mary's choice to believe in Jesus and accept his revelation results from a complex interplay of divine initiative and human response that ultimately effects rebirth. God initiates the process by giving Mary a desire for rebirth. Jesus mediates by revealing God's presence to her. And Mary responds by accepting Jesus as "the Word" and receiving the revelation he offers. Yet these events are not one-time occurrences; rather they represent an ongoing and dynamic interaction between Mary, Jesus, and God.

> Whenever people are in a relationship together, there is a to and fro of energy, desire, and memory. One person's excess may be offset by the other's response; the two continue to respond to each other in some way or another, keeping up a kind of oscillation.[8]

Mary's participation and engagement also are key: she does not spontaneously choose to believe simply because God is revealed to her; she participates in making meaning of the miracle she has witnessed. An event occurs that forces her to see more clearly than ever before the meaninglessness and falsehood of the world in which she lives. Yet, she engages deeply with this event and, once her eyes are opened, it is no longer possible to return to the previous life. The obvious implication is that our faith is continually being shaped and reshaped, and the "trial" of being transformed occurs many times in our lives. We are subjects in process, shaped by an ongoing and dynamic relationship with Jesus and God—a relationship of mutuality, authenticity, and love.

Finally, the contrast between Martha and Mary alerts us to the risks of grasping too tightly the truth claims we hold. Martha is so certain of the truths she has been given that she fails to allow space for new understandings to emerge. Mary, on the other hand, is open, subversive, and willing

---

7. Ward, *Christ and Culture*, 213.
8. McAfee, *Julia Kristeva*, 42.

to be wrong in the pursuit of a truth she can accept at her core. Catherine Keller's concept of theology as "truth-process" is relevant here, reminding us that "the claim of absolute truth is the greatest single obstruction to theological honesty."[9] In addition to being theologically dishonest, absolute truth claims are especially dangerous when they are used as a wall to exclude new ideas, knowledge, or individuals or when they polarize, divide, exclude, or oppress.

The process of reading the John text intertextually with Kristeva's theories illustrates the value of employing new hermeneutical lenses, a practice that allows for the possibility of renewed meaning and renewed truth claims:

> Truth happens in the space opened up in the conversation between newly found dialogue partners—whether those dialogue partners be human interrogators, literary texts, works of art, or cultural artifacts.[10]

Through this kind of dialogue or intertextual reading, we can hope to reach the second naiveté of Paul Ricoeur—allowing us to hear the text anew through dialogue, criticism, and reinterpretation.[11]

---

9. Keller, *On the Mystery*, 8.
10. Ricoeur, *Figuring the Sacred*, 1.
11. Ibid., 6.

APPENDIX
Subjectivity in Psychoanalytic Theory and Rebirth in the Gospel of John

Kristeva's Theory of Human Subjectivity		
The Not-Yet-Subject	*The Developing Subject*	*The New Subject*
• exists in semiotic *chora* • discovers union is not real • abjects maternal figure • opens space for self to emerge	• encounters something other than self • transfers attachment to imaginary father • begins to mimic language of others	• new subject is constituted • acquires symbolic language • enters Social Order

Traditional Understanding of Rebirth in John's Gospel		
Before Rebirth	*Catalyst for Rebirth*	*After Rebirth*
• walks in darkness • is spiritually blind • lives in the world below • rejects Jesus as "the Word"	• believes in/into Jesus • accepts Jesus as "the Word" • receives the revelation Jesus offers • turns away from the world below	• has eternal life • enters the kingdom of God • abides in unity with Jesus/God • lives in the world above

New Model for Rebirth in John's Gospel		
The World as Illusion	*Boundary of Transformation*	*A Radically New Life*
• lives in illusory world of apparent safety • experiences separation or dispossession • moves from security to awakening • moves from insider to Other	• experiences an in-breaking of the Divine • recognizes the illusion of the world • makes new meaning of separation/being Other • experiences the intersection of two realities	• becomes transformed self • gains new identity as child of God • creates community in which Other is welcome • participates in the life of the Divine • experiences abiding divine friendship

Bibliography

Alcorn, Marshall W., Jr., and Mark Bracher. "Literature, Psychoanalysis, and the Re-Formation of the Self: A New Direction for Reader-Response Theory." *PMLA* 100 (1985) 342–54.

Anderson, Paul N. *The Christology of the Fourth Gospel: Its Unity and Disunity in the Light of John 6.* Wissenschaftliche Monographien zum Neuen Testament 2/78. 1996. Reprinted, Eugene, OR: Wipf & Stock, 2010.

———. "Jesus and Transformation." In *From Christ to Jesus*, edited by J. Harold Ellens and Wayne G. Rollins, 305–28. Psychology and the Bible—A New Way to Read the Scriptures 4. Westport, CT: Praeger, 2004.

Bach, Kent, and Robert M. Harnish. *Linguistic Communication and Speech Acts.* Cambridge: MIT Press, 1979.

Bakhtin, Mikhail. "Forms of Time of the Chronotope in the Novel: Notes toward a Historical Poetics." In *The Dialogic Imagination: Four Essays,* 84–258. Translated by Caryl Emerson and Michael Holquist. Austin: University of Texas Press, 1981.

Bal, Mieke. *Death and Dissymmetry: The Politics of Coherence in the Book of Judges.* Chicago Studies in the History of Judaism. Chicago: University of Chicago Press, 1988.

Barrett, C. K. *The Gospel according to St John: An Introduction with Commentary and Notes on the Greek Text.* London: SPCK, 1955.

Beardsworth, Sara. *Julia Kristeva: Psychoanalysis and Modernity.* Albany: State University of New York Press, 2004.

Beavis, Mary Ann. "Mary of Bethany and the Hermeneutics of Remembrance." *Catholic Biblical Quarterly* 75 (2013) 739–55.

———. "Reconsidering Mary of Bethany." *Catholic Biblical Quarterly* 74 (2012) 281–97.

Becker-Leckrone, Megan. *Julia Kristeva and Literary Theory.* New York: Palgrave Macmillan, 2005.

Beirne, Margaret M. *Women and Men in the Fourth Gospel: A Genuine Discipleship of Equals.* Journal for the Study of the New Testament Supplements 242. London: Sheffield Academic, 2003.

Bennema, Cornelis. *Encountering Jesus: Character Studies in the Gospel of John.* Minneapolis: Fortress, 2014.

Black, C. Clifton. "'The Words That You Gave to Me I Have Given to Them': The Grandeur of Johannine Rhetoric." In *Exploring the Gospel of John: In Honor of D. Moody Smith,* edited by R. Alan Culpepper and C. Clifton Black, 220–39. Louisville: Westminster John Knox, 1996.

Bibliography

Brodie, Thomas L. *The Gospel according to John: A Literary and Theological Commentary*. New York: Oxford University Press, Inc., 1993.

Brown, Raymond E. *The Gospel according to John (I–XII)*. Anchor Bible 29. Garden City, NY: Doubleday, 1970.

———. *The Gospel according to John (XIII–XXI)*. Anchor Bible 29A. Garden City, NY: Doubleday, 1970.

Bultmann, Rudolf. *The Gospel of John: A Commentary*. Edited by R. W. N. Hoare and J. K. Riches. Translated by G. R. Beasley-Murray. 1971. Reprinted, Eugene, OR: Wipf & Stock, 2014.

———. *Theology of the New Testament*. 2 vols. Translated by Kendrick Grobel. 1951–1955. Reprinted, Waco: Baylor University Press, 2007.

Butler, Judith. "The Body Politics of Julia Kristeva." *Hypatia* 3.3 (1989) 104–18.

Cahill, P. Joseph. "The Johannine *Logos* as Center." *Catholic Biblical Quarterly* 38 (1976) 54–72.

Clark-Soles, Jaime. "'I Will Raise [Whom?] Up on the Last Day': Anthropology as a Feature of Johannine Eschatology." In *New Currents through John: A Global Perspective*, edited by Francisco Lozada and Tom Thatcher, 29–53. Resources for Biblical Study 54. Atlanta: Society of Biblical Literature, 2006.

Collins, Raymond F. *These Things Have Been Written: Studies on the Fourth Gospel*. Louvain Theological and Pastoral Monographs 2. Leuven: Peeters, 1990.

Coloe, Mary L. *Dwelling in the Household of God: Johannine Ecclesiology and Spirituality*. Collegeville, MN: Liturgical, 2007.

———. "Welcome into the Household of God: The Foot Washing in John 13." *Catholic Biblical Quarterly* 66 (2004) 400–15.

Conway, Colleen. "Gender Matters in John." In *A Feminist Companion to John*, edited by Amy-Jill Levine and Marianne Blickenstaff, 2:79–103. Feminist Companion to the New Testament and Early Christian Writings 5. Cleveland: Pilgrim, 2003.

———. *Men and Women in the Fourth Gospel: Gender and Johannine Characterization*. Society of Biblical Literature Dissertation Series 167. Atlanta: Society of Biblical Literature, 1999.

Cosgrove, Charles H. "A Woman's Unbound Hair in the Greco-Roman World, with Special Reference to the Story of the 'Sinful Woman' in Luke 7:36–50." *Journal of Biblical Literature* 124 (2005) 676–91.

Counet, Patrick Chatelion. *John, A Post-Modern Gospel: Introduction to Deconstructive Exegesis Applied to the Fourth Gospel*. Biblical Interpretation Series 44. Leiden: Brill, 2000.

Culbertson, Diana. *The Poetics of Revelation: Recognition and the Narrative Tradition*. Studies in American Biblical Hermeneutics 4. Macon, GA: Mercer University Press, 1989.

Culpepper, R. Alan. *Anatomy of the Fourth Gospel: A Study in Literary Design*. Foundations and Facets: New Testament. Philadelphia: Fortress, 1983.

———. "Inclusivism and Exclusivism in the Fourth Gospel." In *Word, Theology, and Community in John*, edited by John Painter, R. Alan Culpepper, and Fernando F. Segovia, 85–99. St. Louis: Chalice, 2002.

Daly, Mary. *Beyond God the Father: Toward a Philosophy of Women's Liberation*. Boston: Beacon, 1973.

D'Angelo, Mary Rose. "Women Partners in the New Testament." *Journal of Feminist Studies in Religion* 1 (1990) 65–87.

Danker, Frederick W. *A Greek-English Lexicon of the New Testament and Other Early Christian Literature*. 3rd ed. Chicago: University of Chicago Press, 2000.
Dodd, C. H. *The Interpretation of the Fourth Gospel*. Cambridge: Cambridge University Press, 1953.
Eliade, Mircea. *Patterns in Comparative Religion*. Translated by Rosemary Sheed. New York: Sheed & Ward, 1958.
Elliott, Anthony. *Psychoanalytic Theory: An Introduction*. 2nd ed. Durham: Duke University Press, 2002.
Esler, Philip F., and Ronald A. Piper. *Lazarus, Mary and Martha: Social-Scientific Approaches to the Gospel of John*. Minneapolis: Fortress, 2006.
Feldman, Emanuel. *Biblical and Post-Biblical Defilement and Mourning: Law as Theology*. New York: Yeshiva University Press, 1977.
Freud, Sigmund. *Beyond the Pleasure Principle*. Translated by C. J. M. Hubback. New York: Boni & Liveright, 1920.
———. "Mourning and Melancholia." In *On the History of the Psycho-Analytic Movement Papers on Metapsychology and Other Works*, edited and translated by James Strachey, 237–60. Standard Edition of the Complete Psychological Works of Sigmund Freud 14. London: Hogarth and the Institute of Psycho-Analysis, 1917.
Gambaudo, Sylvie. *Kristeva, Psychoanalysis and Culture: Subjectivity in Crisis*. Ashgate New Critical Thinking in Philosophy. Burlington, VT: Ashgate, 2007.
Gaventa, Beverly Roberts. *From Darkness to Light: Aspects of Conversion in the New Testament*. Philadelphia: Fortress, 1986.
Geertz, Clifford. *Local Knowledge: Further Essays in Interpretive Anthropology*. New York: Basic, 1983.
Grese, William C. *Corpus Hermeticum XIII and Early Christian Literature*. Studia ad Corpus Hellenisticum Novi Testamenti 5. Leiden: Brill, 1979.
Groden, Michael, Martin Kreiswirth, and Imre Szeman, eds. *Contemporary Literary and Cultural Theory*. Baltimore: Johns Hopkins University Press, 2012.
Grosz, Elisabeth. "The Body of Signification." In *Abjection, Melancholia, and Love: The Work of Julia Kristeva*, edited by John Fletcher and Andrew Benjamin, 80–103. Warwick Studies in Philosophy and Literature. New York: Routledge, 2012.
Guberman, Ross Mitchell, ed. *Julia Kristeva Interviews*. European Perspectives. New York: Columbia University Press, 1996.
Haenchen, Ernst. *John 2: A Commentary on the Gospel of John, Chapters 7–21*. Edited by Robert W. Funk with Ulrich Busse. Translated by Robert W. Funk. Hermeneia. Philadelphia: Fortress, 1984.
Hägerland, Tobias. "John's Gospel: A Two-Level Drama?" *Journal for the Study of the New Testament* 25 (2003) 309–322.
Henriksen, Jan-Olav. *Desire, Gift and Recognition: Christology and Postmodern Philosophy*. Grand Rapids: Eerdmans, 2009.
Holland, Norman N. "Unity, Identity, Text, Self." In *Reader-Response Criticism: From Formalism to Post-Structuralism*, edited by Jane P. Tompkins, 118–33. Baltimore: Johns Hopkins University Press, 1980.
Howard-Brook, Wes. *Becoming Children of God: John's Gospel and Radical Discipleship*. The Bible in Liberation Series. Maryknoll, NY: Orbis, 1994.
Hunter, David. "Marginalising the Majority? Theology of the Poor in the Gospel of John." In *Prophecy and Passion: Essays in Honour of Athol Gill*, edited by David Neville, 247–69. Hindmarsh: Australian Theological Forum, 2002.

BIBLIOGRAPHY

Iser, Wolfgang. *The Act of Reading: A Theory of Aesthetic Response*. Baltimore: Johns Hopkins University Press, 1978.

———. *The Implied Reader: Patterns of Communication in Prose Fiction from Bunyan to Beckett*. Baltimore: Johns Hopkins University Press, 1974.

———. "Interaction Between Text and Reader." In *The Reader in the Text: Essays on Audience and Interpretation*, edited by Susan Rubin Suleiman and Inge Crosman, 106–19. Princeton: Princeton University Press, 1980.

———. "The Reading Process: A Phenomenological Approach." *New Literary History* 3 (1972) 279–99.

Keck, Leander E. "Derivation as Destiny: 'Of-ness' in Johannine Christology, Anthropology, and Soteriology." In *Exploring the Gospel of John: In Honor of D. Moody Smith*, edited by R. Alan Culpepper and C. Clifton Black, 274–88. Louisville: Westminster John Knox, 1996.

Keener, Craig S. *The Gospel of John: A Commentary*. 2 vols. Peabody, MA: Hendrickson, 2010.

Kelber, Werner H. "Metaphysics and Marginality in John." In *What Is John?* Vol. 1, *Readers and Readings of the Fourth Gospel*, edited by Fernando F. Segovia, 129–54. Society of Biblical Literature Symposium Series 3. Atlanta: Scholars, 1996.

Keller, Catherine. *On the Mystery: Discerning God in Process*. Minneapolis: Fortress, 2008.

Keltner, S. K. *Kristeva: Thresholds*. Key Contemporary Thinkers. Malden, MA: Polity, 2011.

Kille, D. Andrew. *Psychological Biblical Criticism*. Guides to Biblical Scholarship. Minneapolis: Fortress, 2001.

Kitzberger, Ingrid Rosa. "Mary of Bethany and Mary of Magdala—Two Female Characters in the Johannine Passion Narrative: A Feminist, Narrative-Critical Reader Response." *New Testament Studies* 41 (1995) 564–86.

Koester, Craig R. *Symbolism in the Fourth Gospel: Meaning, Mystery, Community*. 2nd ed. Minneapolis: Fortress, 2003.

———. "What Does It Mean to Be Human? Imagery and the Human Condition in John's Gospel." In *Imagery in the Gospel of John: Terms, Forms, Themes, and Theology of Johannine Figurative Language*, edited by Jörg Frey, Jan G. van der Watt, and Ruben Zimmermann, 403–20. Tübingen: Mohr/Siebeck, 2006.

Kristeva, Julia. *Black Sun: Depression and Melancholia*. Translated by Leon S. Roudiez. European Perspectives. New York: Columbia University Press, 1989.

———. *In the Beginning Was Love: Psychoanalysis and Faith*. Translated by Arthur Goldhammer. European Perspectives. New York: Columbia University Press, 1987.

———. *New Maladies of the Soul*. Translated by Ross Guberman. European Perspectives. New York: Columbia University Press, 1995.

———. "'Nous Deux' or a (Hi)Story of Intertextuality." *The Romantic Review* 93.1–2 (2002) 7–13.

———. *Powers of Horror: An Essay on Abjection*. Translated by Leon S. Roudiez. European Perspectives. New York: Columbia University Press, 1982.

———. *Revolution in Poetic Language*. Translated by Margaret Waller. New York: Columbia University Press, 1984.

———. *Strangers to Ourselves*. Translated by Leon S. Roudiez. European Perspectives. New York: Columbia University Press, 1991.

———. "The System and the Speaking Subject." In *The Kristeva Reader*, edited by Toril Moi, 24–33. New York: Columbia University Press, 1986.

———. *Tales of Love*. Translated by Leon S. Roudiez. New York: Columbia University Press, 1987.
Kristeva, Julia, and Scott L. Malcomson. "Foreign Body: A Conversation with Julia Kristeva and Scott L. Malcomson." *Transition* 59 (1993) 172–83.
Kurek-Chomycz, Dominika A. "The Fragrance of Her Perfume: The Significance of Sense Imagery in John's Account of the Anointing at Bethany." *Novum Testamentum* 52 (2010) 334–54.
Kwok Pui-lan. "Claiming a Boundary Existence." *Journal of Feminist Studies in Religion* 3.2 (1987) 121–25.
———. *Introducing Asian Feminist Theology*. Cleveland: Pilgrim, 2000.
Lacan, Jacques. "The Mirror Stage as Formative of the Function of the 'I,' as Revealed in Psychoanalytic Experience." In *Ecrits: The First Complete Edition in English*, translated by Bruce Fink, 75–81. New York: W.W. Norton, 2002/2006.
Ladd, George Eldon. *A Theology of the New Testament*. Rev. ed. Grand Rapids: Eerdmans, 1993.
Lee, Dorothy. "Abiding in the Fourth Gospel: A Case Study in Feminist Biblical Theology." In *A Feminist Companion to John*, vol. 2, edited by Amy-Jill Levine and Marianne Blickenstaff, 64–78. Cleveland: Pilgrim, 2003.
———. *Flesh and Glory: Symbolism, Gender, and Theology in the Gospel of John*. New York: Crossroad, 2002.
———. "Friendship, Love, and Abiding in the Gospel of John." In *Transcending Boundaries: Contemporary Readings of the New Testament—Essays in Honor of Francis J. Moloney*, edited by Rekha M. Chennattu and Mary L. Coloe, 57–74. Biblioteca di Scienze Religiose, 187. Rome: Ateneo Salesiano, 2005.
———. *The Symbolic Narratives of the Fourth Gospel: The Interplay of Form and Meaning*. Journal for the Study of the New Testament Supplements 95. Sheffield: JSOT Press, 1994.
Levine, Amy-Jill. "John." In *The Women's Bible Commentary*. Exp. ed. with Apocrypha, edited by Carol A. Newsom and Sharon H. Ringe, 381–93. Louisville: John Knox, 1998.
Lincoln, Andrew T. "The Lazarus Story: A Literary Perspective." In *The Gospel of John and Christian Theology*, edited by Richard Bauckham and Carl Mosser, 211–32. Grand Rapids: Eerdmans, 2008.
Maccini, Robert Gordon. *Her Testimony is True: Women as Witnesses according to John*. Sheffield, UK: Sheffield Academic, 1996.
Malina, Bruce J. *The New Testament World: Insights from Cultural Anthropology*. 3rd ed. Louisville: Westminster John Knox, 2001.
Malina, Bruce J., and Richard L. Rohrbaugh. *Social-Science Commentary on the Gospel of John*. Minneapolis: Fortress, 1998.
Margaroni, Maria. "'The Lost Foundation': Kristeva's Semiotic *Chora* and Its Ambiguous Legacy." *Hypatia* 20, no. 1 (Winter 2005) 78–98.
Martyn, J. Louis. *History and Theology in the Fourth Gospel*. Louisville: Westminster John Knox, 2003.
McAfee, Noëlle. *Julia Kristeva*. New York: Routledge, 2004.
Mead, G.R.S., translator. "The Cup or Monad," *Corpus Hermeticum* IV. 11. The Corpus Hermeticum and Hermetic Tradition. The Gnostic Society Library. http://gnosis.org/library/grs-mead/TGH-v2/th209.html.

Meeks, Wayne. "Breaking Away: Three New Testament Pictures of Christianity's Separation from the Jewish Communities." In *To See Ourselves as Others See Us: Christians, Jews, "Others" in Late Antiquity*, edited by Jacob Neusner and Ernest S. Frerichs, 93–115. . Studies in the Humanities 9. Atlanta: Scholars, 1985.

Michaels, J. Ramsey. *The Gospel of John*. Grand Rapids: Eerdmans, 2010.

Miller, Susan. "Mary (of Bethany): The Anointing of the Suffering Messiah." In *Character Studies in the Fourth Gospel: Narrative Approaches to Seventy Figures in John*, edited by Steven A. Hunt et al., 473–86. Wissenschaftliche Monographien zum Neuen Testament 314. Tübingen: Mohr/Siebeck, 2013.

———. "The Woman Who Anoints Jesus (Mk 14:3–9): A Prophetic Sign of the New Creation." *Feminist Theology* 14 (2006) 221–36.

Millgram, Abraham E. *Jewish Worship*. Philadelphia: Jewish Publication Society of America, 1971.

Moloney, Francis J. "Can Everyone Be Wrong? A Reading of John 11:1–12:1–8." *New Testament Studies* 49 (2003) 505–527.

———."The Faith of Martha and Mary: A Narrative Approach to John 11:17–40." *Biblica* 75 (1994) 471–93.

———. *Signs and Shadows: Reading John 5–12*. Minneapolis: Fortress, 1996.

Moltmann-Wendel, Elisabeth. *The Women around Jesus*. New York: Crossroad, 1982.

Moule, C. F. D. "The Individualism of the Fourth Gospel." *Novum Testamentum* 5 (1962) 171–90.

Nissen, Johannes. *The Gospel of John and the Religious Quest: Historical and Contemporary Perspectives*. Eugene, OR: Pickwick, 2013.

———. "Rebirth and Community: A Spiritual and Social Reading of John 3:1–21." In *Apocryphon Severini: Presented to Søren Giversen*, edited by Per Bilde et al., 121–39. Aarhus: Aarhus University Press, 1993.

O'Day, Gail R. "New Birth as a New People: Spirituality and Community in the Fourth Gospel." *Word & World* 8 (1988) 53–61.

O'Day, Gail R., and Susan E. Hylen. *John*. Westminster Bible Companion. Louisville: Westminster John Knox, 2006.

Oliver, Kelly. "The Crisis of Meaning." In *The Kristeva Critical Reader*, edited by John Lechte and Mary Zournazi, 36–54. Edinburgh: Edinburgh University Press, 2003.

———. "Kristeva and Feminism." Feminist Theory, the Center for Digital Discourse and Culture at Virginia Tech University. http://www.cddc.vt.edu/feminism/Kristeva.html.

———. "Kristeva's Imaginary Father and the Crisis in the Paternal Function." *Diacritics* 21.2/3 (1991) 43–63.

———. *Reading Kristeva: Unraveling the Double-Bind*. Bloomington: Indiana University Press, 1993.

Painter, John. "Eschatological Faith in the Gospel of John." In *Reconciliation and Hope: New Testament Essays on Atonement and Eschatology Presented to L. L. Morris on His 60th Birthday*, edited by Robert Banks, 36–53. Grand Rapids: Eerdmans, 1974.

———. "John 9 and the Interpretation of the Fourth Gospel." *Journal for the Study of the New Testament* 28 (1986) 31–61.

Paloutzian, Raymond F., and Crystal L. Park, eds. *Handbook of the Psychology of Religion and Spirituality*. New York: Guilford, 2005.

Payne, Michael. *Reading Theory: An Introduction to Lacan, Derrida, and Kristeva*. Cambridge, MA: Blackwell, 1993.

Philo of Alexandria. *The Works of Philo.* New ed. Translated by C. D. Yonge. Peabody, MA: Hendrickson, 1993.

Plato, *Timaeus.* Translated by Donald J. Zeyl. Indianapolis: Hackett, 2000.

Pollock, Griselda. "Dialogue with Julia Kristeva." *Parallax* 4.3 (1998) 5–16.

Rashkow, Ilona N. "In Our Image We Create Him, Male and Female We Create Them: The E/Affect of Biblical Characterization." *Semeia* 63 (1993) 105–13.

Reinhartz, Adele. *Befriending the Beloved Disciple: A Jewish Reading of the Gospel of John.* New York: Continuum, 2002.

———. "From Narrative to History: The Resurrection of Mary and Martha." In *"Women Like This": New Perspectives on Jewish Women in the Greco-Roman World,* edited by Amy-Jill Levine, 161–84. Early Judaism and Its Literature 1. Atlanta: Scholars, 1991.

Rensberger, David. *Johannine Faith and Liberating Community.* Philadelphia: Westminster, 1988.

Resseguie, James L. *The Strange Gospel: Narrative Design and Point of View in John.* Biblical Interpretation Series 56. Leiden: Brill, 2001.

Ricoeur, Paul. *Figuring the Sacred: Religion, Narrative, and Imagination.* Minneapolis: Fortress, 1995.

———. *Oneself as Another.* Translated by Kathleen Blamey. Chicago: University of Chicago Press, 1992.

Ridderbos, Herman N. *The Gospel according to John: A Theological Commentary.* Translated by John Vriend. Grand Rapids: Eerdmans, 1997.

Robbins, Ruth. *Literary Feminisms.* Transitions. New York: St. Martin's, 2000.

Sayers, Janet. *Divine Therapy: Love, Mysticism, and Psychoanalysis.* Oxford: Oxford University Press, 2003.

Schnackenburg, Rudolf. *The Gospel according to St John.* 3 vols. Translated by Cecily Hastings et al. Herder's Theological Commentary on the New Testament. New York: Crossroad, 1982.

Schneiders, Sandra M. "Death in the Community of Eternal Life: History, Community, and Theology in John 11." *Interpretation* 41 (1987) 44–56.

———. "The Foot Washing (John 13:1–20): An Experiment in Hermeneutics." *Catholic Biblical Quarterly* 43 (1981) 83–87.

———. "History and Symbolism in the Fourth Gospel." In *L'Evangile de Jean: Sources, Rédaction, Théologie,* edited by M. de Jonge, 371–76. Bibliotheca Ephemeridum theologicarum Lovaniensium 44. Leuven: Leuven University Press, 1977.

———. "The Resurrection (of the Body) in the Fourth Gospel: A Key to Johannine Spirituality." In *Life in Abundance: Studies of John's Gospel in Tribute to Raymond E. Brown S.S.,* edited by John R. Donahue, 168–98. Collegeville, MN: Liturgical, 2005.

———. *Written That You May Believe: Encountering Jesus in the Fourth Gospel.* New and exp. ed. New York: Crossroad, 1999/2003.

Schüssler Fiorenza, Elisabeth. *Jesus—Miriam's Child, Sophia's Prophet: Critical Issues in Feminist Christology.* New York: Continuum, 1994.

———. *The Power of the Word: Scripture and Rhetoric in Empire.* Minneapolis: Fortress, 2007.

Seim, Turid Karlsen. "Roles of Women in the Gospel of John." In *Aspects on the Johannine Literature: Papers Presented at a Conference of Scandinavian New Testament Exegetes at Uppsala June 16–19, 1986,* edited by Lars Hartman and Birger Olsson, 56–73. Coniectanea Biblica: New Testament Series 18. Uppsala: Almqvist & Wiksell, 1987.

Smith, D. Moody. *The Theology of the Gospel of John*. New Testament Theology. Cambridge: Cambridge University Press, 1995.
Staley, Jeffrey Lloyd. *The Print's First Kiss: A Rhetorical Investigation of the Implied Reader in the Fourth Gospel*. Society of Biblical Literature Dissertation Series 82. Atlanta: Scholars, 1988.
Sternberg, Meir. *The Poetics of Biblical Narrative: Ideological Literature and the Drama of Reading*. Indiana Literary Biblical Series. Bloomington: Indiana University Press, 1985.
Stibbe, Mark W. G. "The Elusive Christ: A New Reading of the Fourth Gospel." *Journal for the Study of the New Testament* 44 (1991) 19–38.
———. *John as Storyteller: Narrative Criticism and the Fourth Gospel*. Society for New Testament Studies Monograph Series 73. Cambridge: Cambridge University Press, 1992.
———. "A Tomb with a View: John 11:1–44 in Narrative-Critical Perspective." *New Testament Studies* 40 (1994) 38–54.
Story, Cullen I. K. "The Mental Attitude of Jesus at Bethany: John 11:33, 38." *New Testament Studies* 37 (1991) 51–66.
Thompson, Marianne Meye. "The Raising of Lazarus in John 11: A Theological Reading." In *The Gospel of John and Christian Theology*, edited by Richard Bauckham and Carl Mosser, 233–44. Grand Rapids: Eerdmans, 2008.
Tilborg, Sjef van. *Imaginative Love in John*. Biblical Interpretation Series 2. Leiden: Brill, 1993.
Toon, Peter. *Born Again: A Biblical and Theological Study of Regeneration*. Grand Rapids: Baker, 1987.
Trumbower, Jeffrey A. *Born from Above: The Anthropology of the Gospel of John*. Hermeneutische Untersuchungen zur Theologie 29. Tübingen: Mohr/Siebeck, 1992.
Van der Watt, Jan G. *Family of the King: Dynamics of Metaphor in the Gospel according to John*. Biblical Interpretation Series 47. Leiden: Brill, 2000.
Vellanickal, Matthew. *The Divine Sonship of Christians in the Johannine Writings*. Analecta biblica 72. Rome: Biblical Institute Press, 1977.
Ward, Graham. *Christ and Culture*. Challenges in Contemporary Theology. Malden, MA: Blackwell, 2005.
Westcott, B. F. *The Gospel according to St. John*. London: Murray, 1903.
Wink, Walter. *The Bible in Human Transformation: Toward a New Paradigm for Biblical Study*. Minneapolis: Fortress, 2010.
Witherington, Ben III. *Women in the Ministry of Jesus: A Study of Jesus' Attitudes to Women and Their Roles as Reflected in His Earthly Life*. Society for New Testament Studies Monograph Series 51. Cambridge: Cambridge University Press, 1984.
Yamaguchi, Satoko. *Mary and Martha: Women in the World of Jesus*. Maryknoll, NY: Orbis, 2002.
Zimmerman, Ruben. "The Narrative Hermeneutics of John 11: Learning with Lazarus How to Understand Death, Life, and Resurrection." In *The Resurrection of Jesus in the Gospel of John*, edited by Craig R. Koester and Reimund Bieringer, 75–101. Wissenschaftliche Untersuchungen zum Neuen Testament 222. Tübingen: Mohr/Siebeck, 2008.

Index

abiding (μένειν), 3, 5, 25, 28, 53, 87, 88, 92, 106, 124–26, 127, 128
absence, 50–51, 54, 56, 57, 58, 59, 60, 69, 85
alterity, 85, 90–91, 116–17
anointing, 7, 8, 9, 45, 103–24, 130
"born from above," 5, 6, 9, 15–41, 44, 50, 52, 76, 91, 117, 126–27, 129
child/children of God, 3, 15, 16, 17–18, 19, 24, 29, 32, 41, 48, 49, 50, 104–6, 130
chronotope of the threshold, 97
cleansing, 33, 94
cognitive dissonance, 34
collectivism, 53
Corpus Hermeticum, 20, 28
counter-coherences, 42
defilement, 55–56, 91–92, 94, 101, 124
desire, 37, 38, 47, 51, 53, 63–64, 69, 73, 75, 78, 85, 86, 88, 90, 132
divine begetting, 15, 17, 21
divine friendship, 3, 124–26
divine initiative, 22–26, 30, 32, 33, 35, 40, 94, 132
dualism of decision, 5, 123
earthly realm, 2, 7, 18, 22, 23, 40, 93, 94, 101
elusiveness, 58, 65
eschatology, 27
eternal life, 17, 18–20, 21–22, 25, 26, 31, 32, 52, 57, 58, 71, 95, 99–100, 111–12, 117, 125, 127, 130

external focalization, 65–66
foot-washing, 119
Freud, Sigmund, 36–38, 52–53, 59, 64, 89
  "Mourning and Melancholia," 64
  Oedipus complex, 37
  pleasure principle, 36–37
  reality principle, 36–37
God the Father, 85, 87, 88, 91, 94, 97, 98, 101, 106, 115, 116, 122, 123, 124
Habdalah ceremony, 121–22, 124
heavenly realm, 2, 7, 17, 18, 19, 22, 40, 93, 94, 101
historical-critical method, 22
identity, 4, 9, 11, 12, 26, 29, 37, 38, 39, 41, 44, 49–51, 56, 60, 62, 63, 81, 90, 103, 104–6, 124, 127, 130
impurity (*tum'ah*), 55–56, 92
individualism, 53, 124, 125
Johannine community, 29, 31
judgment (κρίσις), 21, 53, 67, 99, 101, 131
kingdom of God, 16, 17, 18, 21–22, 24, 29, 30, 31, 115–17, 130
Kristeva, Julia, 8, 9, 35–36, 38–39, 40–41, 44, 46, 47–48, 50, 51–52, 53, 54–55, 59, 61–63, 65, 67–69, 71–76, 79–80, 85–86, 88, 89–90, 91–92, 93, 94, 97, 98, 102–3, 104, 105–6, 107, 112–13, 116–18, 125, 129, 130–31, 133

145

Kristeva, Julia (continued)
    abjection, 8, 38–40, 52–53, 54–57,
        59, 61–65, 85, 89, 91–92, 94,
        105, 116, 122, 126, 131
    imaginary father, 89–91, 94, 105,
        115
    inaugural loss, 64
    intertextuality, 9
    intimate revolt, 112–13
    logic of renewal, 80
    loving imaginary father, 89, 115
    narcissistic crisis, 62
    narcissistic structure, 57, 89
    negativity, 79, 107
    paternal function, 52, 88, 90
    pre-existing maternal law, 52
    primary identification, 90, 105,
        115
    rejection, 79, 80, 107, 131
    semanalysis, 102–3
    semiotic, 48, 68–69, 70, 72–76,
        79, 92, 93, 97, 98, 102, 107,
        112, 117–18, 131
    semiotic *chora*, 38, 40, 41, 44,
        46–48, 51, 52, 53, 61, 68, 79,
        80, 84–86, 101, 128
    signifying process, 47, 73, 74, 76,
        102–3, 118, 131
    speaking beings (*parlêtres*), 47
    stasis, 79–80, 107, 131
    subject-in-process (*le sujet en
        procès*), 39, 75–76, 80, 103,
        116, 130, 131
    subject on trial, 75–76, 131
    subjectivation, 86
    subjectivity, 8, 9, 10, 36, 38–39,
        41, 46–48, 51–53, 54, 60, 61,
        62, 65, 68, 69, 75–76, 79–80,
        85–86, 89–90, 105, 107, 113,
        131–32
    thetic break, 65, 68, 78–79, 80,
        118
    thetic phase, 68
    threshold of language, 68, 128
    transposition, 103, 107
    unconscious bodily drives, 36–37,
        47, 51, 52, 73–76, 79, 85, 102,
        118

Lacan, Jacques, 36–38, 48, 52–53,
    78–79, 85, 89, 94
    desire of the Other, 78
    imaginary, 37–38
    imago, 79
    Law of the Father (*nom-du-père*),
        38, 52, 89, 94
    Name of the Father, 94
    mirror stage, 38, 48, 77–79, 89
Lazarus of Bethany, 9, 41, 43, 44,
    45, 49, 54–55, 57–60, 65–67,
    71–72, 78, 82, 83, 84, 86–87,
    91–101, 104, 106, 111, 114–
    15, 119, 121, 122, 123, 124,
    126, 130
logocentric bias, 76
Logos, 11, 15, 19, 48, 61, 123, 124
loss, 37, 50, 51, 54, 59, 60, 62, 63, 64,
    69, 72, 78, 85, 86, 88, 89, 90,
    130
love commandment, 7, 113–15
Martha of Bethany, 6, 8, 26, 42–46,
    49, 55, 57, 58, 59, 61, 63, 64,
    66, 68, 69, 70–76, 77–78, 82,
    84–85, 96, 104, 111, 129, 132
Nicodemus, 15, 16–17, 19, 26–27,
    29–30, 32, 70–71, 131
origin, 23–24, 26
Other, Otherness, 3, 4, 9, 11, 13, 39,
    61–63, 68, 78–79, 88, 90, 91,
    101, 105, 113, 115–16, 127,
    132
patriarchy, 2, 4, 61–62, 75
Plato, 46
pneuma (πνεῦμά), 16, 17, 18, 19, 23
power (ἐξουσία), 3, 15, 18, 19, 48,
    105–106
profane, 93, 101, 121, 123
psychological/psychoanalytic
    criticism, 8
purifying, 33, 91, 94, 122
regeneration, 16, 28, 30
rhetoric of grandeur, 108
sacred, 91, 92, 93, 100, 101, 121, 123
sacrifice, 9, 93, 94
salvation, 5, 17, 20–21, 24, 26, 27, 29,
    31, 67, 131
sanctifying, 33, 92–94

sarx (σάρξ), 16, 17, 18, 19, 23
second naiveté, 133
Self and Other, 4, 11, 12–13, 39, 63, 68, 127
sensory imagery, 107–8, 110
sign (σημεῖον), 26, 32, 43, 70, 74, 82, 86, 96, 98–100, 101, 102, 103, 105, 111, 121–22, 123, 126
Son of Man, 19, 20, 32
spiritual life, 56, 71–72, 93, 112, 123, 130
subjectivity, 8, 9, 10, 12, 36, 37–39, 41, 46–48, 51–53, 54, 60, 61, 62, 65, 66, 68, 69, 75–76, 79–80, 82, 85–86, 88, 89–90, 94, 99, 100, 105, 107, 113, 115, 116, 121, 124, 131–32
symbol, 7, 8, 10, 20, 27, 29, 32, 38, 51, 98–100, 119–21, 123–24
symbolic, 51, 54, 72, 73–74, 79, 91, 93, 94, 98, 101, 102, 107, 117–18, 120, 124, 131
symbolic language, 47, 48, 59, 68, 69, 73, 74, 75, 85, 89, 117–18
symbolic order/realm, 38, 48, 51, 62, 68–69, 75, 79, 84, 89, 92, 93, 98, 101, 112–13, 117–18
symbolism of the center, 93
textual gaps, 82–83
Timaeus, 46
transcendent, 2, 11, 58, 94, 99, 119, 121, 122
transformation, 2, 5, 6, 8, 9, 25, 26–29, 30–31, 32, 33, 34, 35, 40, 44, 79, 101, 103, 104, 126, 127, 128, 129
two-level drama, 31
unbound hair, 107, 119, 120–21
Word, the, 19, 47–48, 76, 123–24, 129, 132
world above, 2, 40, 52, 58, 66, 94
world below, 2, 40, 52, 60, 66, 80, 94, 100, 129

www.ingramcontent.com/pod-product-compliance
Lightning Source LLC
Chambersburg PA
CBHW051942160426
43198CB00013B/2270